100 Days to Learn Masonic Ritual

A Workbook to Learn Masonic Ritual in 100 Days and Prepare for the Worshipful Master's Chair

Robert Bone

Emulation Ritual Edition

Contents

Introduction

Hello, I'm Robert Bone, and welcome to your workbook to get you ready for being Installed into the Worshipful Master's Chair of your Masonic Lodge.

Before going any further I must point out that I'm not an expert by any means. I'm not a trained actor who has memorised the works of Shakespeare, neither am I a memory expert, or even a Freemason with decades of experience and the Master of many Lodges. I did, however, have the desire to perform the Ritual well during my year as Worshipful Master of my Lodge.

The fact you have purchased this workbook shows you too are committed to performing to the best of your ability.

I joined Kennet Lodge (in the Province of Berkshire, in the UK) in 2008 and was installed as Worshipful Master in in 2015. This quick ascent through the offices was more to do with member resignations, rather than talent on my part.

When I was voted Master Elect I wanted to try and document my time in the Chair so I set up a website, *www.in-the-chair.co.uk,* where I blogged about meetings and any tips for prospective Masters.

It was on this blog that I started writing about my 100 day plan which forms the back-bone of this workbook. The idea being each day I would work on a certain part of the ritual, and others could follow along via social media.

I also set up, produced and presented the UK's only (at the time of writing) Masonic themed podcast, also called *In The Chair.* The podcast is aimed at Freemasons of all levels, but is also perfectly suitable for non-Freemasons to listen to. You can subscribe via iTunes or listen through the website, *www.masonicpodcast.com.*

By all accounts I am an average Freemason.

However, I do try to take pride in whatever I attempt to do, and I wanted to give being Master of my Lodge my best effort. I'm sure we've all seen Ritual performed that has made us cringe, and thought to ourselves that we want to do a better job when it is our turn. I needed to start learning!

Dipping into the Ritual book wasn't working, and picking certain larger pieces meant I was missing out on much of the smaller parts that bind a ceremony together. I soon realised I was going to have to start putting some structure to my Masonic learning.

So why should I create this workbook, and what skills and techniques can I impart on the Master Mason?

For the past ten years I have been a full time professional magician (entertaining at weddings, corporate events and the occasional Ladies Night – see *www.robertbone.co.uk*). Although sleight of hand has no use in Freemasonry, a few other skills I've learnt along the way can utilised.

The first thing other Freemasons think is because I perform I am good at learning scripts. My performance (both on stage and when mingling) involves a lot of interaction so it's more a case of ad-libbing between bullet points, not word-for-word recitals as required in Freemasonry.

I assume you aren't a professional magician, but it's likely that anyone who has given a speech or sales presentation (even if just to one person) will use a similar process of conveying information, and parts of this can be applied here.

Another element I use is memory techniques. During my cabaret show I give a demonstration of memory techniques – in fact I once memorised the position of every card in a shuffled deck!

Again, I'm not expecting you to be a memory expert; but as I had already explored this area I knew these techniques existed and therefore researched in greater detail to distil those methods most applicable to the average chap struggling to learn a page full of words. Surprisingly some of these methods you may already use in other parts of your life; you just don't realise it, nor applied these methods to your Masonic learning.

Regarding this aspect I very strongly recommend you read *Learning Masonic Ritual* by Rick Smith. Rick's book goes into more detail with the specific details and techniques involved, as well as the "three phases" of learning which this workbook utilises to aid learning.

It can be purchased either as a book or downloaded onto your Kindle, and using the link *www.in-the-chair.co.uk/learning* will redirect you straight to the Amazon page.

Rick was also kind enough to talk about it on episode three of the *In The Chair* podcast (listen at *www.masonicpodcast.com/3*), it's one of the most listened to episodes.

I'm a great believer in improving a little bit every day. Improving by just 1% each day is easily manageable and only takes you ten to twenty minutes, but over time the results compound; and the quality will be better and more easily retained by this sustained repetition.

Hopefully you can see that I really am just an average Freemason, but one that wanted have pride in their work. By the mere fact you have this workbook in your hand demonstrates you are too.

Good luck, and please let me know how you get on

Fraternally yours,

Robert Bone, February 2017
robert@in-the-chair.co.uk

How to Use This Guide

This workbook (note 'workbook', not 'book') is split into two parts.

The first part goes over some fundamental hints and tips for learning Masonic ritual. This includes some of the basics in learning techniques, as mentioned in the introduction I thoroughly recommend *Learning Masonic Ritual* by Rick Smith, available via *www.in-the-chair.co.uk/learning* for a more detailed look at the techniques used in this book.

The second part is the hundred day study guide, which makes up the backbone of this book.

If you are a Master Mason working through the Offices then I recommend reading this first part now, then coming back to the workbook section 100 days later.

Let's address a few points:

Aim of This Workbook

This workbook is not designed to get you from complete novice to word-perfect Worshipful Master in 100 days. It is expected that:

- You have already held Offices in your Lodge,
- You have attended a Lodge of Instruction and/or Lodge rehearsals whilst a Master Mason,
- You want to perform to the best of your ability and realise it will take some work and commitment.
- You will commit 10 to 20 minutes each day - and stick to it!

If that's case, this workbook will:

- Make you fully prepared and rehearsed for your Installation Ceremony,
- Give you a solid grounding for performing First, Second and Third Degree ceremonies during your year in the Chair.

By putting in place a strict regime of structured learning and utilising methodical techniques you'll be amazed at what you can achieve over the course of the next hundred days.

9

It doesn't take too much time either. If you can average 15 minutes each day to work through that day's learning you'll have put in 25 hours of solid learning.

Some days may require a little more time than others, and I've tried to make it so that tougher days are followed by a less strenuous one.

Regardless of exact time spent, doing a little for a hundred days will give you much better results than attempting to learn and rehearse a full ceremony in just a week or two.

Type of Ritual, and Lodge Variations

This edition of the workbook assumes that you are the Master Elect of a Craft Lodge in the UK which practises Emulation Ritual. I am fully aware that there are different types of Ritual not just around the world, but also in the UK. This workbook focuses on Emulation for the following reasons:

1. Emulation is the most popular ritual in the UK,
2. Other workings (both in the UK and Internationally) are based on Emulation,
3. This guide is written based on my own personal experience of preparing to go into the Chair of my Lodge, which is an Emulation one.

If you are a member of a Lodge that practises a different working then just apply a little common sense. Similarly, I appreciate even Lodges that officially practise Emulation still have their own versions and "Lodge Workings". Your Lodge workings may require additional work that isn't contained in this workbook so be sure you allocate extra time for it.

This workbook doesn't give the precise Ritual you should be able to follow along regardless of Ritual differences.

Should your version of Ritual be completely different then the lessons still apply, and you can still use it as a guide to create your own 100 day plan.

Edition of Ritual Book

During the course of this workbook I have used the page numbers of the 13th Edition of the Emulation Ritual as published by Lewis Masonic. This is available in both the pocket sized version, as well as the larger print version (which I highly recommend, see *www.in-the-chair.co.uk/large*). It should also be noted that whilst the typeface is different to ease reading in the large print version, the layout and page numbers are the same.

This is the most common edition of the Emulation Ritual books in use in the UK today.

Of course, older members will have older editions where the page numbers do not match those given in this workbook. It is likely that members who have one of these editions will have already passed though the Chair.

Should you have an older (or future) edition of Ritual book or you work different workings I have also been careful to ensure that title of the piece is clear and describes the Ritual for that day's learning. Therefore you should still be able to follow along in your book, simply ignore the quoted page numbers.

The Master's Work

Although the book of Emulation Ritual dictates that pretty much everything is performed by the Worshipful Master, in reality quite a lot is outsourced. For example, prayers are usually read by the Lodge Chaplain and the Working Tools presented by a Master Mason or a Past Master.

This workbook makes similar assumptions. Speak to your Lodge Secretary, Director of Ceremonies or a Past Master and ask if your Lodge has any special workings; particularly in the Installation Ceremony.

For example, in my Lodge there is some additional Ritual that explains some unique inscriptions on the Immediate Past Master's collar. Of course, this isn't included in the guide, but I had to allow a little extra time to work on this short piece.

If you've been paying attention in Lodge over the last few years you shouldn't have any surprises.

Making Notes

At the end of each day's session make some notes. Even if it is something as simple as "went well", then it still records the fact you did it. (If you have a digital version of this workbook then use a notepad or diary to make notes, or start a document on your tablet/smartphone for this purpose.)

You may come up with your own memory linking system (more on that later) to remember the order of some words, or perhaps have a memory that helps you recall something. Don't rely on the *"I'll remember that"* method – trust me, you won't.

I knew someone who told me he never takes notes because if something is important he would remember it. The irony is if he forgot something important, how would he know he had forgotten it?

Should you have areas of concern also make note of it. Sometimes there are lines that just don't want to sink in and require a little more dedication. Knowing this upfront will help you plan accordingly when you revisit a piece.

During the course of the hundred days you will be going back over pieces many times and the workbook points out when that last was. Before starting each day flip back to that session to read your notes.

The simple act of logging your process will assist you in building the habit of learning and rehearsing Masonic Ritual.

Ultimately I've tried to make this workbook as usable by as many Master Elects as possible, regardless of your location or Lodge's Workings.

And remember: ***As each day brings you closer to your Installation, each day also increases your Masonic knowledge and confidence in performing the Ritual.***

When is the Best Time to Learn Masonic Ritual?

Many have said to me that first thing in the morning is the best time to learn the Ritual, a then the brain is fresh and ready to absorb. Maybe I'm not a morning person, but I need a little time to wake up first.

Generally, you want to learn when your mind is awake and open, but before it gets cluttered thinking about the day ahead. Personally I find this is about half an hour after I've woken. I'll wake up and have breakfast, then hit the blue book for a quick session once I'm half way through a cup of tea.

Due to time constraints this is normally quite a short session, but then I revisit it again around lunchtime and though it won't be fresh in my mind, it will at least be familiar. I'll try again in the evening, possibly a little either before or after dinner. After that my brain is too tired to learn effectively.

If you could fit in three 10 minute sessions that would total 30 minutes each day. And because your brain would be fresh each time you would likely achieve more in the those sessions then one single half hour session.

As you progress through the workbook and are at the stage of having committed chunks of the Ritual to memory; then you can take advantage of other times in the day to practice, for example when driving or walking the dogs.

These times aren't good for learning when you are constantly looking at the book, but useful for repeating and rehearsing passages.

Where is the Best Place to Learn?

Well, the places go hand in hand with the times.

Make sure you get away from distractions when learning - this is especially important when you are first learning a piece and trying to get familiar with it. Ensure the TV is turned off, as well as the radio or any other source of background noise – especially anything with speech or lyrics.

Turn off your phone or other mobile devices, or leave them in a different room or location out of reach. Not only would getting a call or notification be a distraction, but it also prevents your mind from wandering and suppresses urges to check Facebook or emails. An emergency isn't going to happen in the next 15 minutes.

Personally, I find going to my bedroom a good place to get away from everything, and I can relax and focus my attention on the Ritual in peace and quiet.

Ensure the room is well lit. If it's dark your eyes will get tired quickly, and you'll lose focus and concentration.

No doubt others have suggested you learn Ritual whilst driving, in the shower, commuting or walking the dogs. Whilst this is a good way to utilise your time when you are familiar with the piece and require revision and practise, this isn't recommended for first learning the Ritual as you'll be constantly looking at the book.

Once you've learnt the Ritual you'll need to rehearse it. You may feel self-conscious when speaking out loud, but when driving no one can hear you so now in the car is a perfect place. If anyone does catch a glimpse of you they will assume you are talking on a hands-free phone.

Find what times and places work for you, and try out different times and places and see what sessions give you the best result. You may find that evenings work better for you.

Remember that the best place for you to *learn* the ritual may not be the best place for you to *rehearse* the ritual.

How Long Does it Take to Learn?

Realistically learning the Ritual usually takes seven or eight years of attending Lodge meetings, Lodge of Instruction and working through the Offices.

It is customary for a Master Mason to spend a year or two as a Steward before starting on the ladder of the progressive Lodge Offices. During this time they may perform small parts in Lodge meetings, such as the Working Tools, but generally they are getting used to being a Freemason. Therefore they won't be spending too much time learning Ritual.

Once a Master Mason is Inner Guard they start needing to learn the Ritual, though there aren't too many lines to be learnt. During this time though they should be familiarising themselves with the Deacon's work in Lodge of Instruction.

The workload increases once they are a Deacon, and this is progressive. Once in the Warden's chairs it is noticeable that there is a decline in the workload. This is deliberate so you can spend those Lodge meetings closely observing the Worshipful Master and preparing for your year in the Chair.

With respect to how long should you spend learning the Ritual; it naturally varies with what you've learnt already and your learning abilities. Your ability to learn also improves the more you do it, just like working a muscle.

An 'old hand' could revise and be word perfect with the Second Degree Tracing Board in half the time a new Mason would take to be proficient at learning the First Degree Working Tools.

When following the hundred days in this workbook I recommend spending 10 to 20 minutes for the average Master Mason. If you find you whizz through a day and confident you have 'nailed it' then finish early, if you are having problems then spend a little longer or come back to it again later in the day with a fresh mind.

Make the most of each session, but spending too much time on it when you're tired it usually time wasted.

Some Useful Hints and Tips

Here are a few other hints and tips.

Split Learning Up

Learning the Ritual can fatigue your brain as it requires a lot of mental effort. You can become tired and mentally exhausted; and in that state of mind your brain is not going to be able to retain the information very well. Therefore, instead of one half hour session in the evening try splitting it into two fifteen minute sessions, or three 10 minute sessions.

This isn't always practical so you may need to think imaginatively, such as ten minutes in the morning (when you'd normally read the paper), ten minutes during your lunch hour, and ten minutes at home in the evening. These shorter sessions will not only help prevent fatigue, but may be easier to fit into a busy lifestyle.

Listening In Lodge

When attending *any* Lodge meeting you should never sit back and relax whilst others are performing ritual.

A very common mistake amongst Master Masons is to only focus on the work they are doing and mentally switch off for the rest of the ceremony. The problem then comes next year when they take another office and have no familiarity with the work and must start from scratch. By simply paying attention to what others are saying and doing you will start building the framework of the Ritual in your mind, so even if you don't learn the words yet, you will understand the structure and this will make learning easier.

Once a Master Mason is in the Junior Warden's chair they'll notice the workload is considerably less than that of the Senior Deacon's. This isn't a time to coast, but to pay attention to the Worshipful Master. For example, a good way to do this is with the Obligations; repeat them (in your mind) as so you were the candidate.
If you make a point of actively listening you'll be surprised how much of the Ritual starts sinking in, just like how you know many of the lines from your favourite film or the lyrics of your favourite songs.

Once familiar try and mouth along to the Worshipful Master. The physical activity of moving your lips may be small, but does help.

Physically Practise, and Out Loud

Though you may feel self-conscious doing it (even if you are alone) try to practise out loud. You don't have to 'project' your voice as you would do in the Lodge room, but speaking the words will make learning easier.

If you only learn using your "internal" voice you may find it very different to actually speaking the words out loud using you "external" voice, as your brain hears and interprets them differently. I first found this when answering the Second Degree questions, which I could do perfectly in my mind; but fell to pieces when I attempted to say it out loud for the first time ever in Lodge!

Practise with Others

Make sure you attend all rehearsals and Lodge of Instructions. On a few occasions I have even visited a Lodge of Instruction associated with another Lodge to get some extra practise in.

If your Lodge doesn't have a Lodge of Instruction find a Lodge that does and ask if you can attend theirs. Many Lodges don't have enough Master Masons going through the progressive offices and these are usually done by past-Masters filling the vacancy. Past-Masters may not want to go to Lodge of Instruction, so there is often a spare seat going they'll be more than happy to let you fill it.

Even outside of formal Lodges of Instruction and rehearsal meetings it is worth practising with others on a less formal basis. It may be that a few of the members of your Lodge meet once or twice a month round someone's house to run through the ceremony in their spare room.

An alternative to members of your own Lodge is to make contact with others who are in similar positions in other Lodges and will be going through the Chair in their Lodge around the same time as you.

This can work as a "support group", as you'll all be in the same boat together, but can support each other and attend each other's ceremonies.

Learning and Memory Techniques

As previously mentioned there are whole books written about learning ritual and utilising memory techniques to learn the words.

I'll very briefly summarise my approach here, but this is what worked for me personally; and when it comes to learning methods different styles work for different people.

When learning the answers to the questions for the Second Degree I learnt them in silence, as so preparing for a written exam. When the questions were said to me and I had to answer aloud I pretty much fell to bits.

Someone later suggested creating an audio version of the Ritual by reading the piece to be learnt and recording it on a smartphone. This can then be played back via earphones as you go about your daily tasks. The idea being that your brain will learn the words, much as you learn the lyrics to a song by repeated listens. This didn't work for me.

Next I tried cramming. Basically forcing the words in by constant repetition and hours spent with the "blue book".

I found this method showed the best results, and as I did it more, the quicker I could learn. I liken this to physical exercise; if you decide to start training for a marathon the first few runs will be painful, but as your body gets used to the constant exercise it will get fitter, adapt and slowly you'll be running further and quicker.

I also started to use mnemonics whilst learning, which is something I'd dabbled with in my day job. (I'm a professional magician, and part of my show includes a demonstration of memory techniques.)

Though these systems can be complicated, I found you don't need to go into that much detail to cherry-pick the techniques applicable to learning Masonic Ritual.

The human brain is designed to spot patterns and create associations, and we can use this to our advantage by using mnemonics.

A simple mnemonic you may be familiar with is reciting the colours of the rainbow. Learning the order of seven abstract words is tricky, but the phrase

"Richard Of York Gave Battle In Vain" is easier to remember, and the initial letter of each word easily relates to a colour; giving us: Red, Orange, Yellow, Green, Blue, Indigo and Violet.

It also pays to use phrases, terms, words or initials you may be familiar with or can readily visualise. For example, in one of the Obligations there is the phrase "duly constituted, properly dedicated" which I was also getting muddled. I now think of the magicians David Copperfield and Paul Daniels, whose initials give me the correct order.

Sometimes the initial letters of a phrase may spell a word, or at least give you the consonants into which you insert the vowels of your choosing.

Look for patterns in the text; you'll be surprised how often what appears a random list of words is actually grouped in alphabetical order. Sometimes all but one is in order, and sometimes remembering just that odd-one-out is enough to make the rest mentally fall into place.

Some words have double meanings which you can use to build a mental image. For example, a Worshipful Master said to me that he always had trouble remembering when to use "pledge", and when to say "promise". Both words are interchangeable in regular speech and both start with the same letter. He then remembered that Pledge is a brand of furniture polish, and would visualise spraying and polishing the candidate at those specific stages in the ritual.

These techniques (and more) are expanded in much greater detail in the excellent book *Learning Masonic Ritual* by Rick Smith.

The book also covers other techniques that though didn't work so well for me, may work for you. As I said, different methods work better for different people. This workbook is created from my personal experience you may find some of my suggestions don't work so well for you, but you can easily substitute them with techniques more effective for your learning preferences.

One of the main principles from *Learning Masonic Ritual* is to use three stages of learning; and it is these three stages this workbook is based around, regardless of what memorisation and learning techniques you use.

I have adapted them a little for this workbook, but to summarise them:

- First stage: Learn (Cram the words with repetition and spotting memory hooks and mnemonics)

- Second stage: Revise (get used to remembering, but not worry about being perfect)
- Third stage: Rehearsal (focus on the upcoming ceremony so you can present it to the best of your ability)

Over the next 100 days you will learn and revise everything for the Installation ceremony, plus the three degree ceremonies. You will rehearse the Installation only though, but will have a good working knowledge of the degree ceremonies which you can rehearse in the weeks leading up to them.

Again, I recommend reading *Learning Masonic Ritual* by Rick Smith for more information. It can be found on Amazon, or use the link *www.in-the-chair.co.uk/learn* will re-direct you to the latest version. It can be purchased as a real book or Kindle ebook.

I also interviewed Rick on *In The Chair* (my Masonic Podcast) which you can hear at *www.masonicpodcast.com/2*, and is also available on iTunes and Stitcher.

Remember: there is no quick short-cut to learning Masonic Ritual. You must dedicate time, patience and hard work! But with constant repetition it will become easier.

Lodge of Instruction

Lodge of Instruction isn't where you go to learn Masonic Ritual, it's where you go to *rehearse* it.

Many times I have seen a Master Mason (and we have all been guilty of this) attending Lodge of Instruction and they read their Ritual directly from the Book. Simply turning up and reading from the book is pointless, you had might as well stay at home and do that.

But isn't Lodge of Instruction where you go to learn? Well, yes... And, no.

It's perfectly fine to take your Ritual book into Lodge of Instruction, unlike into an actual Lodge meeting where that would be frowned upon. However, the Ritual book shouldn't be relied on, but used as a tool to prompt and remind the user.

As someone once said to me, "you learn the black ink at home, you come to Lodge of Instruction to learn the red ink." By this he meant the 'stage' directions and how the written words come together into an actually ceremony with interaction between the various officers, the candidate and of course the floor work.

Putting in the time to learn the Ritual you'll be performing can work wonders. At first you'll make plenty of mistakes; but no one expects people to be perfect at Lodge of Instruction, if everyone was there would be no point having it. It is, however, a safe place for you to make mistakes in.

Sometimes the most important lessons we learn come from our mistake and assumptions. Lodge of Instruction is where the knowledge and tips of experienced Freemasons are handed down to younger Master Masons.

Regularly a Lodge of Instruction is interrupted by someone keen to pass their knowledge on. For example, a prospective Deacon may be learning the words of the office from their Ritual book, but describing the methods of moving the candidates from west to east is something best taught visually. Not just the actions, but where to stand to get the right spacing.
The perambulations and interactions with the candidate, Lodge Wardens and the Worshipful Master are easier to learn when physical rehearsing it with others in an actual Lodge room.

Even if you've spent time learning and revising the Ritual ahead of meeting you'll soon find that we all have memory lapses, and having the book to hand is useful in Lodge of Instruction.

Occasionally a person may read from the book to speed the ceremony along, but this shouldn't be a regular occurrence.

It is generally considered better that someone attempts what they've been learning without the book and make errors, rather than read from the book and be right.

Lodge of Instruction is where you go to make mistakes, and humans learn from their mistakes; so make your mistakes there so you don't make them in the actual Lodge meeting.

Calculating Your Start Date

This workbook is designed to cover the 100 days leading up to your Installation into the Chair of your Lodge.

It finishes the day before your Installation, not the day of your Installation – you don't want to be learning, revising and rehearsing on that day!

Over the next few pages find the date of your Installation, the column next to it is the date you start this workbook. That is Day 1 of this guide.

Should there be a leap-year between starting this workbook and being Installed into the Chair then you have a few options. You could either take it into account by starting a day later, or have 29th February as a day off, or use it as a bonus day to work on an area in need of improvement.

If it is over a hundred days until your Installation then I recommend you pop the start date in your diary and spend the time between now and then just reading through your Ritual book and getting familiar with it. Should you spot any memory hooks make a note in the margin so you don't forget.

I also recommend using the time before you start the hundred days to read *Learning Masonic Ritual* by Rick Smith (quick link is *www.in-the-chair.co.uk/learning*) which will fully arm you with all the techniques you'll be using – and more.

There are other books on Freemasonry and general memory techniques that are also worth reading. From a book you may pick up just one or two ideas, but if those ideas turn your Ritual from mediocre to something that connects with a new candidate it is worth the investment.

Ensure you keep up to date with the workbook. It may seem a long time off but a hundred days will pass by quickly, and if you start falling behind it will be hard to catch up again. Don't fall into bad habits.

Make the commitment to yourself to dedicate just 10 to 20 minutes a day to this workbook and you – and those attending your meeting - will be stunned by the results.

Installation Date	Start Date	Installation Date	Start Date
1 January	23 September	1 February	24 October
2 January	24 September	2 February	25 October
3 January	25 September	3 February	26 October
4 January	26 September	4 February	27 October
5 January	27 September	5 February	28 October
6 January	28 September	6 February	29 October
7 January	29 September	7 February	30 October
8 January	30 September	8 February	31 October
9 January	1 October	9 February	1 November
10 January	2 October	10 February	2 November
11 January	3 October	11 February	3 November
12 January	4 October	12 February	4 November
13 January	5 October	13 February	5 November
14 January	6 October	14 February	6 November
15 January	7 October	15 February	7 November
16 January	8 October	16 February	8 November
17 January	9 October	17 February	9 November
18 January	10 October	18 February	10 November
19 January	11 October	19 February	11 November
20 January	12 October	20 February	12 November
21 January	13 October	21 February	13 November
22 January	14 October	22 February	14 November
23 January	15 October	23 February	15 November
24 January	16 October	24 February	16 November
25 January	17 October	25 February	17 November
26 January	18 October	26 February	18 November
27 January	19 October	27 February	19 November
28 January	20 October	28 February	20 November
29 January	21 October		
30 January	22 October		
31 January	23 October		

Installation Date	Start Date	Installation Date	Start Date
1 March	22 November	1 April	23 December
2 March	23 November	2 April	24 December
3 March	24 November	3 April	25 December
4 March	25 November	4 April	26 December
5 March	26 November	5 April	27 December
6 March	27 November	6 April	28 December
7 March	28 November	7 April	29 December
8 March	29 November	8 April	30 December
9 March	30 November	9 April	31 December
10 March	1 December	10 April	1 January
11 March	2 December	11 April	2 January
12 March	3 December	12 April	3 January
13 March	4 December	13 April	4 January
14 March	5 December	14 April	5 January
15 March	6 December	15 April	6 January
16 March	7 December	16 April	7 January
17 March	8 December	17 April	8 January
18 March	9 December	18 April	9 January
19 March	10 December	19 April	10 January
20 March	11 December	20 April	11 January
21 March	12 December	21 April	12 January
22 March	13 December	22 April	13 January
23 March	14 December	23 April	14 January
24 March	15 December	24 April	15 January
25 March	16 December	25 April	16 January
26 March	17 December	26 April	17 January
27 March	18 December	27 April	18 January
28 March	19 December	28 April	19 January
29 March	20 December	29 April	20 January
30 March	21 December	30 April	21 January
31 March	22 December		

Installation Date	Start Date	Installation Date	Start Date
1 May	22 January	1 June	22 February
2 May	23 January	2 June	23 February
3 May	24 January	3 June	24 February
4 May	25 January	4 June	25 February
5 May	26 January	5 June	26 February
6 May	27 January	6 June	27 February
7 May	28 January	7 June	28 February
8 May	29 January	8 June	29 February
9 May	30 January	9 June	1 March
10 May	31 January	10 June	2 March
11 May	1 February	11 June	3 March
12 May	2 February	12 June	4 March
13 May	3 February	13 June	5 March
14 May	4 February	14 June	6 March
15 May	5 February	15 June	7 March
16 May	6 February	16 June	8 March
17 May	7 February	17 June	9 March
18 May	8 February	18 June	10 March
19 May	9 February	19 June	11 March
20 May	10 February	20 June	12 March
21 May	11 February	21 June	13 March
22 May	12 February	22 June	14 March
23 May	13 February	23 June	15 March
24 May	14 February	24 June	16 March
25 May	15 February	25 June	17 March
26 May	16 February	26 June	18 March
27 May	17 February	27 June	19 March
28 May	18 February	28 June	20 March
29 May	19 February	29 June	21 March
30 May	20 February	30 June	22 March
31 May	21 February		

Installation Date	Start Date	Installation Date	Start Date
1 July	23 March	1 August	23 April
2 July	24 March	2 August	24 April
3 July	25 March	3 August	25 April
4 July	26 March	4 August	26 April
5 July	27 March	5 August	27 April
6 July	28 March	6 August	28 April
7 July	29 March	7 August	29 April
8 July	30 March	8 August	30 April
9 July	31 March	9 August	1 May
10 July	1 April	10 August	2 May
11 July	2 April	11 August	3 May
12 July	3 April	12 August	4 May
13 July	4 April	13 August	5 May
14 July	5 April	14 August	6 May
15 July	6 April	15 August	7 May
16 July	7 April	16 August	8 May
17 July	8 April	17 August	9 May
18 July	9 April	18 August	10 May
19 July	10 April	19 August	11 May
20 July	11 April	20 August	12 May
21 July	12 April	21 August	13 May
22 July	13 April	22 August	14 May
23 July	14 April	23 August	15 May
24 July	15 April	24 August	16 May
25 July	16 April	25 August	17 May
26 July	17 April	26 August	18 May
27 July	18 April	27 August	19 May
28 July	19 April	28 August	20 May
29 July	20 April	29 August	21 May
30 July	21 April	30 August	22 May
31 July	22 April	31 August	23 May

Installation Date	Start Date
1 September	24 May
2 September	25 May
3 September	26 May
4 September	27 May
5 September	28 May
6 September	29 May
7 September	30 May
8 September	31 May
9 September	1 June
10 September	2 June
11 September	3 June
12 September	4 June
13 September	5 June
14 September	6 June
15 September	7 June
16 September	8 June
17 September	9 June
18 September	10 June
19 September	11 June
20 September	12 June
21 September	13 June
22 September	14 June
23 September	15 June
24 September	16 June
25 September	17 June
26 September	18 June
27 September	19 June
28 September	20 June
29 September	21 June
30 September	22 June

Installation Date	Start Date
1 October	23 June
2 October	24 June
3 October	25 June
4 October	26 June
5 October	27 June
6 October	28 June
7 October	29 June
8 October	30 June
9 October	1 July
10 October	2 July
11 October	3 July
12 October	4 July
13 October	5 July
14 October	6 July
15 October	7 July
16 October	8 July
17 October	9 July
18 October	10 July
19 October	11 July
20 October	12 July
21 October	13 July
22 October	14 July
23 October	15 July
24 October	16 July
25 October	17 July
26 October	18 July
27 October	19 July
28 October	20 July
29 October	21 July
30 October	22 July
31 October	23 July

Installation Date	Start Date
1 November	24 July
2 November	25 July
3 November	26 July
4 November	27 July
5 November	28 July
6 November	29 July
7 November	30 July
8 November	31 July
9 November	1 August
10 November	2 August
11 November	3 August
12 November	4 August
13 November	5 August
14 November	6 August
15 November	7 August
16 November	8 August
17 November	9 August
18 November	10 August
19 November	11 August
20 November	12 August
21 November	13 August
22 November	14 August
23 November	15 August
24 November	16 August
25 November	17 August
26 November	18 August
27 November	19 August
28 November	20 August
29 November	21 August
30 November	22 August

Installation Date	Start Date
1 December	23 August
2 December	24 August
3 December	25 August
4 December	26 August
5 December	27 August
6 December	28 August
7 December	29 August
8 December	30 August
9 December	31 August
10 December	1 September
11 December	2 September
12 December	3 September
13 December	4 September
14 December	5 September
15 December	6 September
16 December	7 September
17 December	8 September
18 December	9 September
19 December	10 September
20 December	11 September
21 December	12 September
22 December	13 September
23 December	14 September
24 December	15 September
25 December	16 September
26 December	17 September
27 December	18 September
28 December	19 September
29 December	20 September
30 December	21 September
31 December	22 September

Learning the Master's Work in 100 Days

Day 1: Investing the Immediate Past Master

Welcome Master-Elect, it's now *just* one hundred days until you get Installed into the Worshipful Master's Chair of your Lodge.

I know it feels like it's a long way off, but that is the sort of thinking that will get you in trouble as time will fly by quickly. Because of that I made a plan to prepare for my own Installation, and that experience has now become this workbook.

This workbook involves breaking down the Ritual into small bite-sized chunks and having schedule learn, rehearse and get word perfect.

The next one-hundred days will get you fully prepared for your Installation ceremony, as well as get you familiar with the other Degree ceremonies you'll be doing during your year in the Chair.

Each day will focus on a part of the Ritual, and we'll be revisiting it numerous times through-out the course so don't worry about being word-perfect straight away.

You'll start this course by looking at the first Ritual you need to say once you've been Installed, that of Investing the Past Master (page 214 in my book of Emulation Ritual).

Have a few read-throughs and get familiar with the structure of the piece, and the words used. See how much you can recite after just ten minutes.

In my Lodge we have two additional sentences that describe some of the plaques attached to the IPM's collar so I needed to include that in my learning too. Check if you Lodge has any unique workings.

Today's Notes: ....

....

....

Day 2: Investing the Senior Warden

Yesterday was Day 1 and you looked at the first part of the Ritual you need to learn for your Installation, that of Investing the Immediate Past Master. This part is in the Inner Workings so you wouldn't have seen it before your own Installation.

Today you are now looking at Investing the Senior Warden (pages 223-224 in my book of Emulation Ritual). Don't fall into the trap of thinking this is shorter than it actually is. It's easy to assume that. I did.

I had foolishly thought it went along the lines of saying "I invest you with this Jewel", then give an explanation of the jewel based on the Working Tools (which I had already learnt previously) and then finishing with explaining the Senior Warden's duties as per the Opening the Lodge.

Yes, it does have those elements, but the description of the Jewel (actually "insignia" for the Senior Warden) is different to the description given in the Working Tools. There is also the gavel and column. The piece can be broken into:

- Saying who will be SW and presenting them with the Collar
- Explaining the Insignia
- Explaining the Gavel
- Explaining the Column
- Explaining position and duties of SW (which is based on what the SW says during the opening and closing of the Lodge)

Remember you're just getting familiarity with the piece for now.

Today's Notes: ....

....

....

....

37

Day 3: Investing the Junior Warden

Today is third day of this workbook, well done for making it this far!

On the first day you concentrated on investing the Immediate Past Master, yesterday was investing the Senior Warden. Predictably today we are looking at Investing the Junior Warden (pages 224-225 in my book of Emulation Ritual).

Yesterday you realised that there was more to investing the Wardens than you may have at first assumed, but found that by breaking down the passage into the natural components made it easier.

Investing the Junior Warden follows the same format so you can break it down into components too, though it isn't an exact copy. For example, the Junior Warden is invested with a "Jewel and Collar", whereas the Senior Warden was invested with an "Insignia".

Investing the Junior Warden can be likewise broken into:

- Saying who will be JW and presenting them with the Collar
- Explaining the Jewel
- Explaining the Gavel
- Explaining the Column
- Explaining position and duties of JW (which is based on what the JW says during the opening and closing of the Lodge)

There is more to this than though than the Senior Warden's especially when it comes to the duties which are more descriptive.

Today's Notes: ....

....

....

....

Day 4: Investing the Officers of the Lodge

Yesterday was the third day and hopefully you are starting to get in the habit.

On the first day you looked at investing the Immediate Past Master, then investing the Senior Warden, and yesterday investing the Junior Warden.

Don't worry if you haven't learnt investing the Wardens word-for-word, you aren't meant to have; at this stage you are getting familiarity this it.

Today we are looking at investing more of the Officers, what I refer to as the Lodge Admin Team (pages 226-229 in my book of Emulation Ritual) and include:

- Chaplain
- Treasurer
- Secretary
- Director of Ceremonies
- Almoner
- Charity Steward

Don't panic! Over the last three days you have been looking at one investiture per day, and now you are doing six?! Yes, but these six are A LOT shorter than the Immediate Past Master and his Wardens.

In each case the Master is asked whom he appoints, the Master says, "I now appoint you my...", invests with the collar and Jewel, and gives a brief description of the Jewel. There are, however, a few points to remember:

- The Treasurer has been elected, not appointed,
- The Treasurer has an insignia, not Jewel,
- The Chaplain and DC's Jewels are not normally explained.

It would be very easy not to worry about this part too much as you don't need to remember what the Jewels are as you'll be looking right at them when you are explaining them. However, during my year in the Chair I visited quite a few Lodges and was surprised how often the Secretary or DC would give the incorrect collar to the WM to invest an officer with.

Even if handed the correct Jewel it won't necessarily remind you of the correct words in the book, it'll just remind you of the Jewel. (I always found it odd that when learning the Working Tools an elder Lodge member would say you can always look down to see what the tools are. I had no problem remembering what they were, it was remembering the page of text that accompanied them!)

Be aware that for each of these Offices there is optional additional descriptions. Many Lodges stick with the standard short Emulation Ritual descriptions, but some do the extended versions – and sometimes only for certain offices.

Contact your Lodge Secretary and/or Director of Ceremonies to check if your Lodge will require you to learn the extended versions. If so ensure you become familiar with them too, and make a note below of the details so you can refer to it when we revisit these investitures through-out the course.

Hopefully today has been a bit of a change of pace from the last few days where we are looking at shorter pieces (but greater in number) as opposed to the longer piece for the IPM and Wardens.

Remember, you aren't looking to get this word perfect, but you should be able to at least recall what each Jewel is, and the general format of investing these offices.

Today's Notes: ....

....

....

....

....

....

....

Day 5: Investing the Senior Deacon

Over the last four days you have read through and become familiar with investing the Immediate Past Master, the Senior Warden, the Junior Warden, and yesterday the "Lodge Admin Team".

Now you return to investing the progressive Offices of the Lodge, and today it's the turn of the Senior Deacon (pages 229-230 in my book of Emulation Ritual).

The Deacons require more work to invest than the Chaplain, Treasurer, Secretary, Almoner and Charity Steward so focus your attention only on the Senior Deacon in today's session.

Quite a bit of the Ritual to invest the Senior Deacon should be familiar to any Mason who has held that office during their Masonic career. There are a few extra bits (such as the ceremonies the Senior Deacon leads the candidate in and the presentation of the wand) that do require some work, so don't get complacent.

Use the parts that you do already know as 'stepping-stones', and use them as a structure to build the rest of the Ritual around. You'll find this stepping-stone technique very useful as we work our way through this course as you'll often come across parts you have already learnt when you were holding another office in the Lodge.

As an additional exercise, if you have a spare ten minutes later today it's a good idea to run through what you've been learning over the last few days. A little refresher once now and again doesn't hurt.

When I tried this I surprised myself by my accuracy, but there were hesitations and a handful of times when a quick glance at the book was needed; but only a couple of times when my brain froze completely. Most of the problems were in the investing of the Junior Warden (the longest piece learnt so far) so I knew I needed to spend some extra effort on it.

Make sure you make a note of any areas where you drew a complete blank so you can ensure you focus on them when you revisit it again.

Don't worry about being word perfect, even if you had to ad-lib parts but conveyed the essence of the piece and used certain key words it demonstrates you are gaining familiarity with the Ritual.

Over the course of the next ninety-five days you'll be going over of the Installation ceremony a lot more. At the moment you're starting with familiarisation of the Ritual and general learning, then you'll move onto revision and finally rehearsal where you is concentrate on the presentation.

Today's Notes: ....

....

....

....

....

....

....

....

....

....

....

Day 6: Investing the Junior Deacon

Remember this course is to get you word perfect when investing the Officers and Closing the Lodge at your Installation at the end of this hundred day run, and also to get a good grip on the rest of the other rituals for your coming year.

So far we have solely focussed on getting familiar with the investiture of your officers.

Having a structured learning, revision and rehearsal schedule should give you confidence that you are going in the right direction. You know that you are covering all aspects required of you, and can easily monitor your progress along the way.

Talking of progress, as yesterday you got familiar with investing the Senior Deacon, it naturally falls that today you'll be looking at investing the Junior Deacon (pages 230-231 in my book of Emulation Ritual).

Just like how the Junior Warden required a little more work than the Senior Warden; again, the Junior Deacon requires a little more work that the Senior Deacon. But as before, it follows the structure of the preceding investiture.

Just like yesterday quite a bit of the ritual for investing of the Junior Deacon should be familiar to any Mason who has held the office during their Masonic career.

Again, there are a few extra bits such as the Junior Deacon attending to the Candidate in the Initiation ceremony, as assisting the Senior Deacon in the other two ceremonies, but the structure of the Ritual follows the same format of the Senior Deacon's.

Be wary of the last sentence about "care and attention" though. It is very similar to the last sentence in the investing of the Senior Deacon, but slightly different. (It's quite ironic that you need to pay care and attention to get it right.)

You could probably say the same sentence for both Senior and Junior Deacon and no-one will bat an eyelid, ad if they do they probably won't pass comment. That said, you're putting this work in to get this right, and those that do know these pieces are normally the Provincial Executive who attend a lot of Installations so appreciate seeing the Ritual performed correctly.

Whilst here take a moment to look at investing the Assistant Director of Ceremonies and Assistant Secretary (if your Lodge has these offices).

The Assistant Director of Ceremonies doesn't have any ritual (unless your Lodge uses the optional extended versions), and the ritual for the Assistant Secretary is the same as the Secretary's, which we covered on Day 4.

You shouldn't need to learn anything new for these two offices, but they get invested immediately after the Junior Deacon and it pays to be familiar with all aspects of the ceremony. You don't want to seize up when you are asked who you'll be investing as your Assistant Director of Ceremonies or Secretary!

Today's Notes: ....

....

....

....

....

....

....

....

....

....

Day 7: Investing the Inner Guard

It has now been a week since you started this one-hundred day plan to learn the ritual before going into the Chair of your Lodge.

Over the last six days you've gone from investing the Immediate Past Master through to the Junior Deacon, and hopefully you are getting to grips with the format of the Installation ceremony.

Today is looking at Investing the Inner Guard (pages 232-233 in my book of Emulation Ritual).

Fortunately the Inner Guard work is quite short and it follows the regular format you are probably getting used to.

The duties should be familiar with too, from either holding this office previously or just listening to what gets said in every Lodge opening. Do bear in mind this isn't exactly what the Inner Guard says in the opening, so again don't get complacent and thing you can wing it, but you should have a passing familiarity with it to use as a foundation.

If you have time see how you get on with what we've been through already over this last week. No doubt you'll need plenty of prompts, but you'll be surprised what you've learnt already.

Remember to make a note of any areas that didn't come to you once you'd given yourself a prompt.

Today's Notes: ....

....

....

....

Day 8: Investing the Tyler

Having completed the investiture of the Inner Guard yesterday there is just one more officer that requires their Jewel. Today you are Investing the Tyler (sometimes known as the Outer Guard, pages 234-235 in my book of Emulation Ritual).

Investing the Tyler is a little longer than the Inner Guard, and the majority of place and duties is taken from the Lodge opening, but again, the duties are a little more expanded and not directly lifted from the text we hear at every Lodge opening.

It's easy to go zooming through the parts you know and then miss the extra out; or worse, have a long pause followed by a prompt in the ceremony; simply because you overlooked it during your preparations.

As well as the text of the Ritual ensure you are familiar with actions required in presenting the sword to the Tyler, the book gives directions to which hands to use and the orientation of the sword. You'll probably have a chance to practice it in a rehearsal ahead of the actual ceremony, but by then you want to be focusing on how you delivering the ritual, not juggling a heavy sword.

So, that's the last part of the Installation ceremony you will need to learn (the rest is done by the newly invested IPM and other Lodge members). We started with investing the IPM on page 214, and finished with investing the Tyler on page 235.

That's over twenty pages of ritual covered in just eight days. Look at what you have achieved so far and realise that at this steady and constant pace you will be fine.

Today's Notes: ....

....

....

Day 9: Closing the Lodge

Over the previous days you have read through everything you (as the newly installed Master) will need to know for the Installation ceremony itself; that is investing the Officers into their respective offices in the Lodge, presenting them with their Jewel and explaining their duties.

Once you've been installed into the Worshipful Masters chair and you've appointed your officers there is still the matter of running the rest of the meeting and Closing the Lodge.

In theory this should be a breeze. This is what you hear at the end of every Lodge meeting you have ever attended. The problem arises when you think you are familiar with it so don't give it much thought in your preparation. Suddenly you're stood at the front of the Lodge, the Installation ceremony is over, you take a deep breath as you realise that all eyes are on you; and you realise you didn't learn what to do next.

Therefore, Day 9 is Closing the Lodge (pages 54-65 in my book of Emulation Ritual).

Remember, as you've just finished the Installation the Lodge is still in the Third Degree. However, it's unlikely that you'll be closing the Third and Second Degrees in full at the Installation, but will be Resuming the Lodge in them (page 68 in my book).

Replacing the Closing in the Third and Second with Resuming definitely reduces the workload, but please don't skip over this. It's only one line but it's important to get it right.

If it is customary for your Lodge to Close is all Three Degrees at the Installation meeting then don't worry as it will be covered during this workbook, but feel free to have a look through them today. Much of the additional work required to close in full is done by the Wardens anyway.

As Master you will also need to go through the rest of the items on the agenda, as well as run any ballots that may be required. Make sure you are familiar with these processes in your Lodge. The best method for this is to pay attention to the Worshipful Master whilst you are still a Warden.

Also, spend some time learning the correct way to do the Risings in your Lodge. The Ritual book gives a guide, but I strongly suggest checking with the secretary or current Master of your Lodge to get the correct wording as some Lodges combine the Risings into one.

Once the ceremony is over and the Lodge is closed you may need to introduce the National Anthem (usually just the first verse) and Closing Ode, and instruct the Organist as appropriate.

Today's Notes: ....

....

....

....

....

....

....

....

....

....

....

Day 10: Investing the IPM and Wardens

You're now a tenth of the way through this hundred day plan to learn Masonic ritual. It's only a small fraction of it, but by taking small bite-sized chunks each day you can see the progress you have made.

So far you have read through everything you (as the newly Installed Master) will need to know for the Installation ceremony, that is installing the Immediate Past Master, Wardens, Deacons and all the other Officers; then Closing the Lodge (before no doubt heading to the bar for a well-earned drink!)

Unless you're superhuman – or spent a few hours each day working at it – I'm guessing you're at the stage where you are getting comfortable with the Installation ceremony and what you need to say, but still have plenty pauses and parts that require looking at the book. Don't worry, that's why it's a hundred day plan, not a ten day plan.

Personally I found that by this stage I wasn't where I had hoped I would be. If you're thinking the same my best advice is *don't panic!* There's a long way to go and everything we've been doing so far has been to get familiarity with the text, anything you've learnt along the way has been a bonus.

Now that you are familiar we are going to pick the pace up and go back to Days 1, 2 and 3, and look again investing the Immediate Past Master (page 214 in my book of Emulation Ritual), the Senior Warden (pages 223-224) and Junior Warden (pages 224-225).

When I went through this myself there were some passages that looked completely alien – almost as if they had been magically added since I had last looked at those pages. I'll run through my experiences up to this point so you can use my experience as a bench-mark for your own.

In the main I was about 75-85% correct (or at least close to enough to demonstrate knowledge). I surprised myself by how much I knew, but there were still a pauses, omissions and occasional glitches.

As soon as I allowed myself a prompt by glimpsing the first couple of words each sentence would pop instantly into my head, but I just couldn't seem to think of them without the initial prompt, even just minutes after I had learnt them. Very frustrating!

I'd say I was also 75-85% with the Senior Warden address. Again, I was happy with this progress as many of the mistakes were of the "right words, wrong order" variety.

The biggest problem I had by this stage had been with the Junior Warden investiture, where I was only about 60-70% with it.

It was good to know I was having these issues this far in advance, and not in the week leading to my Installation.

The investiture of the Junior Warden is the longest passage of all the offices to be invested. Much of it is based on the same format as the Senior Warden, and some of the extension is merely including the line "and your brother Senior Warden" in places. However, a couple of times I thought I'd nailed it only to realise that I had missed out the entire part about examining visitors!

Focus your attention today on your problem areas and make a note of them for future work, but do not neglect the rest of it.

Try writing out any lines you have problems with, then pinning it somewhere prominent so you can cast your eye over them through-out the day.

Today's Notes: ....

....

....

....

....

....

Day 11: Investing the Lodge Officers

Onto day eleven of this hundred day plan to learn Masonic ritual. I hope you're glad we started when you did because time does go by quickly.

You are now working your way through the Installation Ceremony (at least, the part you need to learn as the newly Installed Master) for the second time and yesterday you looked at investing the Immediate Past Master and your two Wardens.

Today is a big day and you will be covering a lot. Seriously, it's a lot. You will have another look at all the remaining Officers (page 226-235 in my book of Emulation Ritual). There are:

- The Chaplain
- The Treasurer
- The Secretary
- The Director of Ceremonies
- The Almoner
- The Charity Steward
- The Senior Deacon
- The Junior Deacon
- Inner Guard
- Any Assistants or other Offices
- The Tyler

Yes, that's a lot we are covering today, but don't expect yourself to be 100% on all of this by the end of today's session. What you are doing is re-familiarising yourself with it, looking for patterns and generally trying to cram as much into your brain as you can through constant repetition.

Also keep vigilant for areas that need work. Don't get angry and beat yourself up if there are parts that you have forgotten, by finding these areas of weakness now you can concentrate on getting them right over the coming weeks.

By far the largest of these addresses are the two Deacons. The others, though numerous, are shorter and tend to follow a format. Some don't even have ritual and only require the Worshipful Master to present the Jewel and say a few words to the individual.

If possible try and split today into different sessions, perhaps have two or three goes at running it through. You may find that what comes easily one time may not so the next. Make a note of areas that you have recurring issues with.

I found I had more sticking points with the Junior Deacon, but not enough to be worried about at this stage of proceedings. To be far though, none of them were absolutely bang on.

Remember, at this stage it is fine if you aren't word perfect or have pauses or need a prompt from your Ritual book. You are still in the learning stage of this process, you'll be coming back to it again and again (and again) to ensure your competency in it.

If you are finding that much of this looks brand new to you and you're relying on reading larger sections (as opposed to smaller prompts) to get you through a passage then it may be you need to consider allocating more time each day to the course, or perhaps have an additional shorter session later in the day.

Don't feel too bad, we all learn at different speeds and what works for one doesn't always work for another. The reason we will be repeating this over and over is to enable you to make a small advancement each day and compound it.

This will also enable you to discover which technique works best for you.

Keep up the good work, and tomorrow isn't so intensive.

Today's Notes: ....

....

....

....

....

Day 12: Resuming and Closing the Lodge

Since you started you have now gone through the Installation ceremony (at least the parts the Master Elect needs to learn) twice. You'll likely be far from perfect; but you should have a good grip on it.

There are probably parts you don't know, but at least you are now aware that you don't know them; and if pushed could have a pretty good stab at guessing. Even if you don't recall the words you should know the structure and that "this is the sentence about…"

The last few days have been pretty intense with yesterday covering A LOT of investitures.

Today you will take another look at Closing the Lodge, you first covered it on Day 9. Most Installation ceremonies will Resume in the Second and First Degree (page 68 in my book of Emulation Ritual), before going through the Lodge business and then Closing (pages 62-65).

Just because these are bits you've heard at pretty much all Lodges you have ever attended and probably said yourself in Lodge of Instruction, do spend the time to ensure you are familiar with it. You don't want to invest your officers perfectly then forget how to Close properly.

Again, also ensure you are familiar with the format you Lodge's agenda (though it's unlikely you'll have the actual Summons yet this far ahead) and the Risings. The Ritual book only gives the basic template, but each Rising has its own way of being said in each Lodge. Don't make assumptions!

If you're happy with the Resuming and Closing you can now choose one of the following options:

1. Pat yourself on the back, put the kettle on and have a cup of tea, pleased that today was a shorter session than the previous days, or,
2. Whilst you're here with the Ritual book to hand have another run through of the Installation, or,
3. Look through your notes and focus your attention on specific areas of the Installation you've identified as needing additional work.

Hopefully you aren't sick of the Installation by now. Don't worry, you aren't spending all of the 100 days just doing the Installation, but it still needs more work before we move on to the Degree ceremonies.

If you chose the second or third options and went through the Installation again make sure you make notes of any areas you are having problems. Also make sure you note any positives, mnemonics, memory hooks or other tips you come up with during the process.

Today's Notes: ....

....

....

....

....

....

....

....

....

....

....

Day 13: Investing IPM and Wardens

You been through the Installation Ceremony twice now (including Resuming and Closing) so you should now be quite familiar with the Ritual and how the parts you need to learn are structured.

Now you will go over it again, but this third time should get you competent with the Ritual.

It still isn't expected that you will be anywhere near perfect yet. The aim now is to get to the stage where you may need the odd glance or prompt, and there may be a few pauses whilst you need to think. Do not worry about presentation or how long your pauses are – take as long as you want.

Today we are going back to the beginning again, and going back over investing the Immediate Past Master, and the Senior and Junior Wardens. You went through these on Days 1, 2, 3 and again on Day 10. Look back over your notes from these days to see if you had any problems you need to focus on, or memory aids you found useful.

As these are the first pieces of Ritual you'll be doing when you are Installed it is likely your brain is going to be all over the place at this point – mine was, I needed three prompts to remember the first line for Installing the Immediate Past Master, despite all the preparation! You will want to make sure that Investing IPM and Wardens is really locked down, so that your mouth can go into auto-pilot whilst you settle into the Chair.

You are now entering the revision phase of the process.

By this stage you should have the book open on the page (in my book Investing the IPM is on 214, Investing the Senior Warden is pages 223-224, and Investing the Junior Warden is pages 224-225), but covered with a piece of paper.

Only reveal the text once you have passed that section to check your accuracy, or when you need an occasional prompt. Don't rush, give yourself a generous amount of time; you'll be surprised what you can remember by waiting a few extra seconds.

If you are still drawing a blank try to take a guess. Finally have a glimpse to prompt yourself. You'll often kick yourself at how close you are.

I found that sitting back, closing my eyes and mouthing along quietly worked quite well, and I could almost visualise the page in front of me. I also found saying it out loud (although barely audibly) helped.

This is because you are turning visual information (the written word) into auditory information, therefore giving your brain another angle of attack and another medium to back up. Also, some people recall information they hear easier than information they read, making this technique invaluable to them.

Of course, you aren't getting to the stage where you'll be performing this in Lodge just yet – you are looking to demonstrate you can recall the Ritual, not perform it

When you get to a sticking point repeat the line a couple of times, really paying attention to the wording. Then go back a couple lines and start repeating from there, notice how the words that you knew fluently lead into the part you had problems with. Repeat this a couple more times, then repeat the whole part again.

Remember to note these problem areas, as well as the solution you found for it for future reference as it's likely you'll have that problem again. Sometimes just acknowledging a problem is enough.

Once you've worked you way through Investing these Offices, go back to the beginning and start again. Your focus should be on accuracy.

By the end of this session aim to be about 85-90% accurate with the Ritual. The performance may be laboured, but you have eighty-eight days to work on that.

Today's Notes: ....

....

....

....

Day 14: Investing Officers and Closing

You are now two weeks into this 100 Day Study Plan to learn Masonic ritual. Isn't it amazing how quickly the time flies? There's still eighty-seven days until the Installation, and as long as you've been putting in sufficient work each day you should be quite pleased with what you have learnt over the last couple of weeks.

Repeating what I said yesterday; the aim now is to get to the stage where you may need the odd glance (or prompt), and accept there may be a few pauses whilst you need to think. Essentially you are packing all the information into your brain, the revision and rehearsal will neaten it up and focus on the details.

Yesterday you started your third run through of the Installation ceremony with the investiture of the Immediate Past Master and the two Wardens. This means you are now in the revision phase of the process (not the learning phase where you first absorbed the bulk of the information, nor the rehearsal phase where you'll be working on the presentation of it.)

Today you will bring the rest of the investitures together and combine it with the Closing of the Lodge. We first covered this on Days 4 to 9, and then again on Days 11 to 12. Look through your notes on these days for any reminders you made.

You will want to have the Ritual book open on the page you are working on, but covered with a piece of paper which you move down as you progress. (In my book Investing the Officers is on pages 226-235, Resuming is on page 68 and Closing the Lodge is pages 62-65.)

Repeating my "getting competent" techniques from yesterday, I found it best to sit back, close my eyes and mouth along quietly. Saying out loud (although barely audible) helps, it's important not to just do the Ritual internally, even if just moving your lips to 'mouth along'.

Run through the Ritual. You may even visualise the page (some people almost take a mental photograph of the page and read from this mental picture, whereas others cannot use this method at all – it varies). Should you encounter parts you get stuck on take a moment to relax and normally the words will magically pop into your head.

If after pausing you are still drawing a blank and take a guess before taking a glimpse of the Ritual. Sometimes your guess will be more accurate then you'd think, demonstrating that you have learnt the Ritual, it's now the recall that needs working on.

Focus your attention on the problem areas (you aren't aiming for perfection, we are looking at the places you fell down on here) and repeat them a couple of times. Re-start a couple of sentences back so you have momentum when you get to it again.

I realise that today's session is quite a long one, but if you have time try going through it again. Preferably this will be in a second session later today so that your subconscious has time to process all this revision and refresh itself.

By the end of today your aim is to be about 85-90% accurate. The performance may be laboured as you are still concentrating on getting the information correct in your head, you still have plenty of time to work on presenting it.

As ever, ensure you keep notes of both successes and failures for future reference. Sometime the act of writing something down is enough to build a neural gateway in your memory.

Today's Notes: ....

....

....

....

....

....

Day 15: Investing IPM and Wardens

Since starting this workbook you have now been through the Installation ceremony (at least the parts the Master Elect needs to learn) three of times.

Hopefully there are parts you have nailed, but it's likely there are still some parts that have that annoying habit of slipping your mind. Fingers crossed these should be in the minority, and you should know where they are in the Ritual; and so you know where to focus your efforts on.

You should be getting to the stage where you are about 85% confident on the Ritual. Today we go back to the beginning (again!) and work on revising investing the Immediate Past Master the he Senior and Junior Wardens.

Yes, I realise you only did this two days ago (Day 13), but before you move on to the other ceremonies you really need to make sure this is properly learnt before moving on.

If you are getting bored of it that's a good sign, it means that you are familiar with it and know it. That ultimately means that it is getting archived in your long-term memory, as opposed to being temporarily stored in your short-term memory.

Before getting over-confident and moving on to the Degree ceremonies you need to make sure the Ritual stays in your long-term memory, and that is achieved by repetition. If you move on now you run the risk of forgetting what you've learnt over the last two weeks.

It is better to be bored learning Ritual now than stressed trying to re-learn it in the week leading up to your Installation ceremony.

With this stage of revision you'll still want to have the Ritual book to hand for easy reference (in my book Investing the IPM is on 214, Investing the Senior Warden is pages 223-224, and Investing the Junior Warden is pages 224-225).

Try and say the ritual without looking at the book at all. If you get stuck just pause, take a breath and let the words come to you – normally they will. It is better you take a stab at it and get it slightly wrong than look at the book too quickly.

After every few sentences check with the Ritual book to ensure you are correct, you don't want to be revising a mistake without even realising it.

If you find you are stuck, miss parts, or can't take an educated guess then go back to learning it. It may be you just need to really focus on a specific sentence.

For a real problem area write that particular part out fifty times, just like doing 'lines' in school detention. After the fiftieth repetition it will be a lot easier to remember.

By the end of this session I want you to feel about 95% confident with Investing the Immediate Past Master and the Wardens. Don't worry about how long it takes to go through or how smoothly it flows; the main objective is to be able to demonstrate you can recall it with accuracy.

It's still eighty-five days until your Installation ceremony, but I want you to feel that if it was next week you'd be able to have a good bash at it.

Keep up the good work, and keep sticking with it. By now you should be in the routine of spending some time each day to learn the Ritual, and worked out when and where works for you and your lifestyle.

Learning Ritual is a skill, and like playing the piano you wouldn't expect to be ready to play a concert after just a few days practise; but you should be adapting to learning a little every day and find your general skill of reading and retaining also improves as each day passes.

You will be covering the Degree ceremonies in this one-hundred day workbook and there are some large pieces of Ritual to be learnt; but by then you'll be so accustomed to learning Ritual it'll be easier as your learning skills develop.

Today's Notes: ....

....

....

....

Day 16: Investing Officers and Closing

Hopefully by now you're seeing that spending a bit of time each day in a coordinated way is making this quite a painless process.

Continuing from yesterday's session (starting the fourth run through of the Installation ceremony) you should now be getting competent with the Ritual. We will complete the investiture of the rest of the Officers and Close the Lodge, essentially repeating Day 14.

Again, have the Ritual booking open on required page of the piece you are revising, but avoid looking. (In my book Investing the Officers is on pages 226-235, Resuming is on page 68 and Closing the Lodge is pages 62-65.)

Like yesterday, if you get stuck just pause, take a breath and let the words come to you – normally they will. It's better at this stage to guess and be slightly wrong than look at the book.

Getting close to correct is better than needing a prompt. It's easy to feel annoyed if you fail to remember parts; but actually you should take it as a boost of confidence that although you may not be 100%, you have enough of a grasp to take a punt at it, and probably be pretty close.

To repeat yesterday's tip, if you find you are stuck, miss sections, or can't take an educated guess then go back to learning it by writing that piece out fifty times. This physical repetition will really help force that pesky bit of Ritual in!

By the end of today's session you should feel about 95% confident with completing the Installation of your Officers and Closing the Lodge. At this stage I still had issues but a prompt would get me back on track.

Today's Notes: ....

....

....

Day 17: Revising The Whole Installation

Over the last 16 days you have been learning the various parts of the Installation ceremony, and started to pull them together into larger and longer sections. Now you are going to combine everything you have done so far into one.

Before starting though make sure read through your notes of all the previous days. This way you know where to concentrate your efforts to make the most use of your time.

It's quite a lot to do but don't be daunted, and feel free to split today into smaller sessions if that's easier for you. It may be wise to have one single run through first, then allocate a little time later today to address parts you felt didn't go as smoothly as you would have liked.

You are still not expected to be word perfect at this yet. I suggest opening the blue book to the required page of the piece, but try and keep it covered whilst you revise. In my book Investing the Officers starts on page 214 with the IPM, then picks up with the Senior Warden on page 223, through the Offices to page 235, then Resuming is on page 68 and Closing the Lodge is pages 62-65.

Try and get through as much of it as possible without looking. Make a note of areas that you need help with, if necessary skip over that piece so you don't get out of the flow, then reviewing these parts in more detail afterwards.

If in doubt have a guess and see how close you are. I'm willing to bet that you were pretty much there, a case of "the right words, the wrong order" and would have at least been able to communicate the sentiment of the line.

Ensure you keep track of where you are in the book and reference it every couple of sentences. It is very easy to get caught in the flow and miss whole chunks out without realising it, especially with the Wardens. (The Junior Warden in particular for me!)

If possible have someone follow along with the book in their hand. Ask them only to give a prompt when you ask, and only offer a correction if you are making a big mistake or missing text. A correction at every minor error or prompt at every short pause can be very distracting, especially at this stage of learning when you are not looking for perfection or presentation.

After you have finished the piece they can highlight any minor errors such as missed words, substituted words or grammatical mistakes.

By the end of this session I would hope you will be about 95% accurate, and you still aren't worrying about the presentation.

Ensure you make a note of any parts you are still having an issue with, or any tips or memory hooks you have discovered to help you recall any specific parts of the Ritual.

This draws a close to the initial learning and revision for your Installation ceremony. Over the coming weeks this workbook will come back to it numerous times refresh this knowledge to keep it current, before giving it that final polish in the week prior to the ceremony.

Treat yourself to a cup of tea, you've earnt it!

Today's Notes: ....

....

....

....

....

....

....

....

Day 18: Opening and The First Degree

So far this workbook has concentrated solely on preparing you for your Installation into the Chair of your Lodge. The objective of this course isn't just to get you ready for that ceremony, but give you a working knowledge of the three Degree ceremonies you are likely to be performing whilst you are in the Chair.

Today we are going to look at Opening the Lodge and the start of the First Degree Ceremony.

There is quite a bit to this and when creating this workbook I first considered spreading this over two sessions, but decided that you should be quite up to speed with the Opening the Lodge (in my book of Emulation Ritual it's pages 42-46) as you've witnessed it in every ceremony you've attended since your own Initiation.

Going through the Offices in your Lodge you will have learnt much of the Ritual involved yourself without even realising it. Rarely to Lodges stick directly to the Ritual book for the opening (mostly getting all the Officers to explain their roles, and some even summon the Tyler in) so ensure you are aware of any specific workings in your Lodge.

Don't be complacent. Just because you've seen it many times, and probably even been in the Chair during Lodge of Instruction; it still pays just to read through it and make sure you know it.

Now the Lodge is open move onto the First Degree ceremony. Work your way gently through this and today just look at admitting the candidate through to the Prayer (pages 69-72). In most Lodges this is done by the Chaplain so you don't need to learn it, but if prayers are said by the Worshipful Master in your Lodge then learn it today.

Most of the work on these pages is done by the Inner Guard and Tyler, although your input is needed, the main part in checking the candidate is suitable, then asking him to kneel.

It's the start of the ceremony so you want to start off on confident footing. You can concentrate on pacing it and start the ceremony feeling relaxed as you ease into it.

Remember this is the candidate's first steps into Masonry, and they will be feeling nervous. If they hear your voice sounding relaxed and confident they will relax and enjoy the ceremony. Give the candidate a ceremony to remember for the right reasons!

The Master who Installed me hadn't learnt the Ritual to the best of his ability. Unfortunately my overriding memory of my Initiation was him nervously stammering through the ceremony and requiring so many prompts that he ended up having to read parts. It is that memory that drove me to ensure the candidates I initiate didn't suffer the same negative experience.

Today's Notes: ....

....

....

....

....

....

....

....

....

Day 19: First Degree Perambulations

Yesterday you started learning the ceremony for the First Degree. You aren't looking to get this word perfect at this moment in time, but to get to grips with what your lines as Worshipful Master are, and how they fit in with the work of the other officers involved in the ceremony.

Having opened the Lodge; the candidate has now been admitted and the Prayer said, now it's the First Degree Perambulations (in my book of Emulation Ritual it's pages 73-77).

When I was in the Master's Chair for a Lodge of Instruction it was these smaller parts of transitional work where I became a bit unstuck.

Without a pre-planned study guide in place you naturally gravitate to learning the larger pieces of Ritual, such as the Obligations, Working Tools or Charges. Often these "transitional" parts are given a cursory glance.

This workbook ensures these smaller pieces of ritual get the due care and attention they deserve. Do not assume that today is an easy day. Put the work in and ensure you are up to speed with this; not just with the words but also the actions, such as when to gavel.

Take it up to the line where you say you will attend to the Senior Warden's presentation but must first ask some questions.

If you do find this quite an easy day then have a revision on yesterday's and let the two parts flow together. Some of the coming days will be require quite a lot of work so don't start coasting now.

Today's Notes: ....

....

....

....

Day 20: First Degree Declarations

You are now a fifth of the way through the workbook. Not a massive slice of the 'Ritual pie', but when you look back over what we have already covered during the last twenty days you see that you will be up to speed with everything by the time of your Installation.

No doubt your ability to read and retain Ritual is improving too, making the process of learning easier.

Yesterday you looked at the Ritual around the First Degree Perambulations. It is easy to dismiss this as the work of the Deacons and Wardens, but actually quite a bit of input is required by the Master as those Officers are following the Master's directions.

You got as far as saying you have a few questions for the candidate - which are the First Degree Declarations (in my book of Emulation Ritual it's pages 77-78).

It's only three questions spread over two pages but they can be problematic for many. The length and format of each of the First Degree Declarations are similar, but small differences make them tricky to learn.

If you find them problematic just spend your time going over and over them again and again, perhaps even writing them out in full a few times each.

With repetition familiarity will follow, and once you have familiarity with a piece you start noticing those small subtleties and patterns that make learning easier. Make sure you note these down for future use.

Don't be worried about getting this perfect yet, get familiarity with the Declarations so you can build upon them throughout this learning process.

Today's Notes: ....

....

....

Day 21: First Degree Pre-Obligation

Today you will continue your first run through of the First Degree ceremony, getting familiar with the format of the Ritual.

Yesterday you focussed on the Declarations, the three questions put to the candidate. Today is another day of 'transitional' Ritual in the First Degree and goes between the Declaration questions and the Obligation (in my book of Emulation Ritual it's pages 78-80).

Today the candidate will be brought up to the pedestal and prepared for the Obligation. The text you must learn for this part includes what must be the funniest line in the Ritual - that apparently Freemasonry is free! It is then a matter of remembering your left from right. The candidate in this degree kneels on their left knee, it's useful to remember this by recalling that when walking in the Lodge everyone starts with their left foot, and as the candidate is starting their Masonic journey they are starting 'by the left'.

Compared to some previous days this isn't too intensive, but there is still quite a chunk of work needed to be done today. As you can probably guess we have the Obligation itself coming up.

Because the Obligations are often regarded the centre-pieces of the Master's work during the ceremonies you know the eyes of the Lodge, and any visitors, will be on you; and you will likely feel the pressure to recite the Obligation to the best of your ability.

Therefore it is important to make sure you learn the work leading up to the Obligation well. This will give you a smooth run up to it, enabling you compose yourself, relax and build your confidence before the Obligation.

Today's Notes: ....

....

....

Day 22: First Degree Obligation

We are really starting to get stuck into the First Degree ceremony now, and yesterday we concluded with the candidate in front of the Worshipful Master's pedestal and prepared for the First Degree Obligation.

This is a large piece of ritual (in my book of Emulation Ritual the First Degree Obligation is on pages 81-83) so be prepared to spend a little extra time today. Don't worry too much though as today we are really focussing on getting familiarity with the piece, rather than attempting to learn it all word-for-word in just one session.

This one hundred day course is to get you word perfect for your Installation seventy-nine days away, and assuming the following month's ceremony will be an Initiation, the soonest you will need to actually say the Obligation in Lodge won't be for another hundred and ten days.

However, spending time now in preparation means you can spend the weeks leading up to the First Degree revising and rehearsing it – not learning.

Read through the Obligation and get familiar with the format and parts. I recommend breaking it further down into more logical bite-sized chunks. Either pencil some back slashes (/) in your Ritual book, or even re-type or re-write it out yourself.

In Emulation Ritual, I suggest breaking the Obligation into the following defined sections:

1. Introduce the Lodge and VSL,
2. What they are promising to do,
3. Who/where they can communicate,
4. The list of methods of writing, and on what,
5. That it shouldn't be readable by anyone,
6. The points they swear to observe,
7. Why they shouldn't violate the Obligation,
8. Finish

I repeat, you aren't attempting learning the entire Obligation today as we'll be coming back to it through-out this workbook. Read it through slowly and adsorb the words and format.

As you work through make notes on any mnemonic links you think of which will aid learning and recalling it at a later date. For example, to aid remembering the phrase "worthy, worshipful and warranted Lodge" think of the three w's at the start of a website address. (The First Degree Obligation is the only Obligation where the 'www' mnemonic can apply.)

If you have large-print Ritual book you may find it useful to also make notes in the margin there too.

Remember, you have at least 110 days (probably longer) until you are performing this for real!

Today's Notes: ....

....

....

....

....

....

....

....

....

....

Day 23: First Degree Obligation – Again!

You are almost a quarter of the way through this hundred day workbook, and you have learnt and revised what you'll be needing to say at your Installation and about half way through the First Degree. This still gives you plenty of time to get familiar with the other two ceremonies.

Make sure you aren't getting left behind though. It is very easy to go back to previous parts you have covered that you feel need more work, but doing this can compromise the current work as you slowly get more and more behind.

If there are areas we have covered that you feel need more work it is better that you make a note of it and keep up to date rather than start falling behind – this workbook allows for this and you will be going over all of it many more times during this process.

Yesterday was the First Degree Obligation. It is a big – and important – piece of ritual to learn. Now, I know I said you are just getting familiarity with the First Degree at the moment, not necessarily trying to get word perfect straight away; however, being such a key piece of Ritual you are going to go through it again today. In my book of Emulation Ritual the First Degree Obligation is on pages 81-83.)

It is a very important piece of Ritual, and the eyes of the Lodge will be on you for it. You also owe it to the candidate to do this well as it is an experience they will remember forever, so make it good.

I recall at my Initiation the Worshipful Master had not learnt the piece adequately. He's a very good Mason but didn't put in the necessary time and effort, and on the night this compounded with his nerves. All I remember is him stumbling, getting prompts and corrections on every line of the Obligation.

During the Obligation it is really the first time the candidate really has a chance to relax and focus on what's going on around them. When the candidate enters they are nervous, their senses heightened whilst they are whisked around the Lodge room by the Junior Deacon.

It is a shift of gears, it gives the candidate a moment to absorb the surroundings and get a sense of what I happening to them. When learning Ritual it helps to keep in mind you are creating an experience for others, not merely reciting words from a book.

Because the candidate is repeating it themselves you need to be speaking it clearly and of a good pace for the candidate to absorb and repeat it back to you. As you are reading through the Obligation break it into even smaller chunks than yesterday and mark them clearly in your Ritual book – this is where you pause so the candidate can repeat it back to you.

Don't expect to get the Obligation down word for word today, but by the end of today's session you should at least know the structure of the piece (look back to yesterday for the guide) and pick out key words and phrases in each section you can use as stepping stones as you work your way through it.

Today's Notes: ....

....

....

....

....

....

....

....

....

Day 24: First Degree Post Obligation

You have now spent two days working on the First Degree Obligation, and yesterday you took some time to consider why this is such an important piece of Ritual, especially from the Candidate's perspective.

After some of these larger chunks of Ritual you have been covering over the last week you will be pleased to know it is a less strenuous session today, as you now look at some more 'transitional ritual' that links the Obligation to the Lesser Lights (in my book of Emulation Ritual this is on pages 83-84).

This transition starts with two small paragraphs (sealing the Obligation and predominant wish of their heart), a longer paragraph explaining the three great lights, before finally asking the candidate to rise.

Regarding the three great lights, although the Ritual used here is unique; the explanations echo the descriptions use in the Working Tools so if you've learnt those previously you'll no doubt recognise the connections which will assist your learning.

As said before, if you don't have a structured plan in learning it is very likely that you'll skip over some of these smaller parts.

Now you are getting used to learning on a daily basis this shouldn't be to arduous. Remember, you are not attempting to be anywhere near knowing it word-for-word at the moment; but to get familiarity with it.

Today's Notes: ....

....

....

....

....

Day 25: Lesser Lights, Dangers and Penalty

You are now a quarter of the way through this workbook and that represents a significant amount of time you have dedicated in learning it.

If you spent on average 20 minutes per day on this plan then you already put in over 8 hours of work, and in that time you are pretty much ready (bar a couple of rehearsals) for your Installation Ceremony, Opening and Closing the Lodge; and got a pretty solid foundation of the First Degree.

Yesterday you sealed the Obligation, restored the blessing of light and explained the great lights in Freemasonry. Now candidate it brought to the side of the pedestal for you to explain the Lesser Lights.

As this is only a sentence long (though it is a long sentence!) so you will also include the dangers that awaited the candidate and the penalty associated to the Obligation (in my book of Emulation Ritual this is on pages 85-86).

One of the first things you'll notice in this the red ink, which are the "stage directions" of the Ritual script. These are quite easy to follow but don't ignore them.

Try to ensure that the directions are followed and acted out, especially in Lodge of Instruction and rehearsals. You don't want to lose your flow when the IPM reminds you of an action that you should have taken.

Being familiar with these actions ensures that you can continue with a steady flow, letting your hands do what they have practised, whilst your mouth gets on with saying the words it has rehearsed.

In this part, and upcoming parts, there are numerous blank spaces and initials in the Ritual that require substitution, if you are in any doubt as to what they are speak to a Past Master as soon as possible and ensure you learn the correct wording. Don't make an assumption and get it wrong.

Today's Notes: ....

....

Day 26: First Degree Entrusting

It has been a busy week learning some large chunks of First Degree Ritual, and today is no exception!

We are now onto learning the First Degree Entrusting (in my book of Emulation Ritual this is on pages 86-89). I initially considered splitting this up as it is quite a lot to do in one session however I decided not to because the piece does have a flow to it.

Another reason I haven't split this is because the last part (the word, and its meaning) should be familiar to you if you've spent time as the Junior Deacon in your Masonic career.

Like yesterday there are quite a few initial letters describing the sign and token. You should be able to work these out, but if you have ANY doubt speak to your Lodge Mentor, current Worshipful Master, or anyone else who can confirm these parts for you correctly.

As ever make sure you record anything you aren't sure of so you can refer back to it in the future.

There is again a fair bit of red-ink in the Ritual book today, which are the 'stage directions' and actions you need to perform. Although you aren't at the stage of rehearsal yet, still read these get familiar with what you need to do. You may finding acting these parts (or at least visualise doing them) assists with learning.

On the bright side, once the candidate has been Entrusted you can hand him over to the Junior Deacon and have a breather whilst he and Wardens do their work!

Today's Notes: ....

....

....

Day 27: First Degree Apron

Yesterday covered a large amount of Ritual with the First Degree Entrusting (which took you up to page 89 in the Emulation Ritual book), after which the Candidate would be handed over to the Junior Deacon for testing by the Wardens.

You can relax a little whilst they do their work, and we pick it up again for the presentation of the First Degree Apron and go through to the Junior Deacon placing the candidate in the North-East part of the Lodge (in my book of Emulation Ritual this is spread over pages 94-96).

Remember there is a short sentence to delegate to the Senior Warden to invest the candidate with the badge, this is a little buried in the Senior Warden's work so take care not to miss this out. It can come as quite a surprise if you have accidentally skipped learning this brief sentence.

The main bulk of the Worshipful Master's work here follows the Senior Warden and Deacon's work, and involves explaining to the candidate when he is to wear the Apron (or more importantly when he shouldn't) and why.

I will remind you again that you are not expected to get word perfect at this stage of the study programme. Don't start repeating days, or trying to fit two days of study into one. This hundred day workbook is designed to slowly build your knowledge through repeated repetition.

Ensure your time is spent reading through and repeating, either out loud, or at least quietly mouthing along. After a couple of times try working your way through with the text covered and see how close you are. Even if you haven't got the words bang on, hopefully you have the sentiment behind each sentence.

Today's Notes: ....

....

....

Day 28: The Charge in the North East

You have now covered the majority of the First Degree, though this is more of an exercise in getting familiar with the Ritual, and the format of the ceremony and how the larger pieces of Ritual can be broken down into manageable parts.

In yesterday's session the Candidate was Invested with the Badge, and it was further explained to him, finishing with moving the Candidate to the North East part of the Lodge.

You now resume with the Charge in the North East (in my book of Emulation Ritual this is on pages 97-98), but only up to the point where you ask the candidate to leave his donation with the Junior Deacon.

The Charge in the North East (that you are looking at today) is two paragraphs, but looking at it you'll see they are long. It will greatly help when learning to break these paragraphs down into smaller parts, similar to how you broke down the Obligation.

I recommend breaking it down into the following sections:

1. Explanation of the cornerstone, and that the candidate represents it,
2. That they now stand upright (just the single sentence),
3. You'll be testing their principles,
4. Explanation of charity,
5. All walks of life in Freemasonry,
6. Test their principles by asking for a donation.

There are also a few unusual words and phrases used in this piece (just like many other parts of the Masonic Ritual). If you are unsure of the meaning of a word look it up in the dictionary; not only will you have a better understanding of the Ritual, but you are more likely to remember these parts as you put in the extra effort to research them.

Remember to make a note of any words you needed to look up.

Today's Notes: ....

....

Day 29: First Degree Charity

You are now nearing the end of your first read through of the First Degree ceremony. Yesterday you started the Charge in the North East, where you broke two long paragraphs into six shorter sections making them easier to learn.

You then introduced the Junior Deacon to test the Candidate, after which he confirms the candidate had nothing to give. The Master's work now continues and completes the Charge in the North-East with an explanation of why charity is important to Freemasons (in my book of Emulation Ritual this is on pages 99-100).

Like yesterday you can break down paragraphs into more discrete portions. Whereas yesterday was two paragraphs divided down to six sections, you can break today into just three:

1. Congratulate the candidate,
2. The first and second reasons,
3. The third reason.

Because the first reason is short and flows into the second I've grouped them together. The third is longer and runs to the end of the piece.

If you look at this the entire piece it is composed of just three sentences. In fact, one sentence covers all three reasons, and due to the use of grammar and punctuation that single sentence is over 15 lines long and a whopping 106 words!

When breaking Ritual up into smaller sections to aid learning find the natural breaks that are dictated by the flow of the Ritual, not necessarily the grammar of the written word.

The final part can be a bit of a tongue twister, and definitely benefits from inserting your own punctuation to reduce this single sentence down.

Please note that I am assuming that the Working Tools and the Charge After Initiation will be outsourced, it is likely to be if this is your first time as Worshipful Master. Often the Working Tools are done by a Master Mason and the Charge After Initiation given by a past Master of the Lodge.

It may be that if you are doing two First Degrees during your term in office these parts could outsourced the first time, then you do it all yourself the next time.

Check with the Director of Ceremonies of your Lodge, and if it is expected for you to do the Working Tools or Charge after Initiation then ensure you allow some additional time to read through these parts too.

Today's Notes: ....

....

....

....

....

....

....

....

....

....

....

Day 30: First Degree Charter and Closing

As explained yesterday we are assuming that the Working Tools will be outsourced to another member of the Lodge as is customary in many Lodges nowadays, so this workbook skips over that.

We pick it up again at explanation of the Charter of the Lodge, which also includes giving the Candidate the Book of Constitutions and By-Laws of the Lodge; as well as letting the Candidate leave the Lodge to restore himself and return (in my book of Emulation Ritual this is on pages 101-103).

Start this by explaining that the Candidate will need to pay his initiation fees, but before doing so you explain under what authority the Lodge acts. This leads to introducing the Charter of the Lodge.

To aid learning break this paragraph at this point, and start a new one when giving the Candidate the Book of Constitutions and By-Laws of the Lodge.

The final paragraph is short enough and written in a more modern style so shouldn't be much trouble to learn, though the last couple of lines may need a couple of additional read-throughs to make it flow naturally.

Because the Charge After Initiation is also usually given by a Past Master who isn't holding an Office this year we are skipping over that and going straight to Closing the Lodge (pages 60-65). Of course, we have already covered Closing the Lodge when preparing for your Installation ceremony.

That concludes the first reading through of the First Degree ceremony, so you should have a good idea of what is expected of you, how you will interact with the candidate and the other officers of the Lodge, and have a solid understanding of how the larger pieces of Ritual can be broken down.

Today's Notes: ....

....

....

Day 31: Installation Ceremony Revision

After almost two weeks of the First Degree Ceremony you are going to have a day of revision of the Installation Ceremony. It's been a while since you learnt this so you'll likely be rusty and forgotten some of what you had learnt. But hopefully the bulk of it had been slowly absorbed into your long term memory.

You will be going through everyone you will need to be saying in the Lodge room during your Installation. This starts in my Ritual book with Investing the Officers on page 214 (with the Immediate Past Master), then picks up again with the Senior Warden on page 223, through the Offices to page 235, then Resuming is on page 68 and Closing the Lodge is pages 62-65.

It was Day 17 when we last revised the Installation Ceremony so take a moment to read through your notes before jumping straight in. You may also find it beneficial to skim through it first as a quick refresher.

Try and get through as much of it as possible without looking for a prompt, making a note of areas that you need help with then skipping over that piece so you don't get out of the flow. Review these parts again afterwards.

If in doubt have a guess and see how close you are. It will likely be a case of "the right words, the wrong order", and you would have at least been able to communicate the sentiment of the line using some of the key words or phrases.

I hope that you were pleasantly surprised with how much you have retained over the last few weeks and it shows that putting in regular study on a daily basis is building your Masonic knowledge.

If there were any parts you feel warrant particular attention write them out and place them somewhere you can look at regularly, such as next to your computer monitor or telephone, or even in the bathroom!

Today's Notes: ....

....

....

Day 32: Opening and Starting the First Degree

Yesterday you mixed things up a little by throwing in a quick revision of the Installation Ceremony. Hopefully you found that you still retained quite a bit of knowledge of the Ritual even though it had been almost two weeks since you were last looking at it.

Today go back to the beginning of the First Degree by opening the Lodge (pages 42-46 in my book of Emulation Ritual), then going through the First Degree ceremony up to the Obligation (pages 69-80). When we first started learning the First Degree it was broken up over four days:

Day 18 – Opening the Lodge in the First Degree and Candidate Enters
Day 19 – Perambulations
Day 20 – Declarations
Day 21 – Pre-Obligation Ritual

Have a look back at those days in this workbook and read your notes. Did you make any tips or jot down any memory hooks? Are there areas you had difficulty with the first time around?

You are still in the learning stage of this so don't worry about testing yourself and trying to be word perfect. Feel free to have the book open, but instead of just reading and repeating, try and see if you can pre-empt what the next line will be.

I found that I couldn't have done this with-out the book open, but once I had taken a prompt from the book I could usually complete the part with a good degree of accuracy. There were areas that need more work, and some that even with a prompt to kick-start still didn't help.

If you have areas of difficulty spend additional time on them, and try repeating them out loud. This is putting it into your short-term memory, but as long as you acknowledge these areas of weakness, come back to them and repeat the process it will eventually build in the long-term memory.

Today's Notes: ....

....

Day 33: First Degree Obligation

You are now a third of the way through the workbook. Looking at what you've covered already, and what's still left to learn, I bet you're glad you started when you did!

Today you'll focus solely on the First Degree Obligation (pages 81-83 in my blue book of Emulation Ritual). On your first reading through you spent two days on this and realised how important it is to do well; not just for the fellow members watching, but also for the Candidate's lasting memories of his first experiences into Freemasonry.

At the start of today's session you may be able to work your way through the Obligation requiring a lot of prompt from the book with perhaps the odd section that you can run through, but by the end of today you won't be perfect but will at least be able to work your way through with a few pauses and only the odd quick peek of your Ritual book.

Each time you go over it you'll notice how it becomes a little easier, and a little more sinks in. At this stage repetition is the key. In a twenty minute session you should be able to read through the First Degree Obligation three or four times. Not skim over, but properly read and absorb it.

Remember you are still in the Learning stage of the First Degree where you are putting the Ritual into your short-term memory with brute force – your subconscious will do the work of moving it into your long term memory with repetition over time.

Today's Notes: ....

....

....

....

Day 34: Lesser Lights and Entrusting

I apologise now, because you will cover A LOT of material today. You'll be going from the end of the First Degree Obligation up to the start of the Charge in the North East (pages 83 to 96 in my book of Emulation Ritual). This covers:

Day 24: Post Obligation
Day 25: Lesser Lights
Day 26: Entrusting
Day 27: Investing with the Badge

This spreads a whooping fourteen pages in my book of Emulation Ritual. This does of course include work for the Junior Deacon and Wardens, but the majority of the work is done by the Master at the Pedestal.

Build up familiarity by repetition. That doesn't mean you can just skim read, but make an effort to read aloud (or at least under your breath) and retain the words, repeating sentences and testing yourself.

As there is a lot to cover today you may find yourself pushed for time. If that is the case then ensure you make a note of any parts that you feel still need additional time, then you can ensure this problem areas are given adequate attention in the future.

By the end of today your familiarity with the First Degree ceremony will have increased as it starts sinking into your long term memory.

Today's Notes: ....

....

....

....

....

Day 35: Charge in the North East

After covering fourteen pages worth of Ritual yesterday we are slowing it down today and just covering the Charge in the North East (pages 97-100 in my book of Emulation Ritual). However, this is a very solid chunk of Ritual as we are now including testing the candidate and the explanation of charity.

You covered this on Days 28 and 29, so as it was just a week ago you may expect it to be quite easy. This will unlikely be the case and you may feel that you are almost starting this piece from scratch.

The Charge in the North East can lull you into false sense of security as this first part is only two paragraphs long. Unfortunately each of those paragraphs are cumbersome, and the use of the language is not as concise at it could be. You'll remember each day was broken down into sections, which combine to:

1. Explanation of the cornerstone, and that the candidate represents it,
2. That they now stand upright (just the single sentence),
3. You'll be testing principles,
4. Explanation of charity,
5. All walks of life in Freemasonry,
6. Test principles by asking for a donation,
7. Congratulate the candidate,
8. The first and second reasons for the test,
9. The third reason.

Remember to check your notes from Days 28 and 29 as you may have jotted down a few hints to help you remember the words, and their meanings, to assist you.

Today's Notes: ....

....

....

....

Day 36: First Degree Charter and Closing

Today you will finish your second read through of the First Degree. This doesn't mean to say that you've learnt it, but after working your way through it steadily you should have a good understanding of the structure of the ceremony and your role within it. This will give a good grounding for future revision and rehearsal in the weeks that lead up to the ceremony once you're in the Chair.

Remember that in this workbook we are assuming that the Working Tools and Charge After Initiation will be performed by other members of the Lodge, if this isn't the case in your Lodge please allow extra time to learn it.

Continue with the explanation of the Charter of the Lodge which also includes giving the Candidate the Book of Constitutions and By-Laws of the Lodge; as well as letting the Candidate leave the Lodge and return (in my book of Emulation Ritual this is on pages 101-103).

You are going over what we first went through on Day 30, starting with explaining under what authority the Lodge acts and that the Candidate will need to pay his initiation fees. Break this paragraph at this point, and start a new one when giving the Candidate the Book of Constitutions and By-Laws of the Lodge.

The final paragraph is short enough and written in a more modern style and therefore easier to learn.

Skipping over the Charge After Initiation go straight to Closing the Lodge (pages 60-65). Though you've covered it a few times within this course don't ignore it and take the opportunity to quickly go through it again.

Today's Notes: ....

....

....

....

Day 37: First Degree Ceremony Revision

So far you've been through the First Degree Ceremony twice. Both of these times were learning, but now you are moving onto the revision stage.

In this session you will revise what you last covered on Day 32.

Start the ceremony by Opening the Lodge (pages 42-46 in my book of Emulation Ritual), then going through the First Degree ceremony up to the Obligation (pages 69-80). When you first started learning this it was broken up over four days:

> Day 18 – Opening the Lodge in the First Degree and Candidate Enters
> Day 19 – Perambulations
> Day 20 – Declarations
> Day 21 – Pre-Obligation

Try to go through this without looking at the book, well, at least not until to you need it. However, don't ignore the book completely and regularly check to ensure you what you've learnt it correct. Use a piece of paper to cover the book and reveal the text once you have worked your way through it.

When you get to a point that you get stuck, stop and think about it. Don't rush yourself. If you are still stuck slide the paper down and reveal the first line to prompt yourself. No doubt there'll be occasions when you kick yourself for not remembering it, and hopefully not too many where the line still doesn't prompt you to continue.

The priory of revision is to recall what you have learnt. You aren't looking for smooth delivery, so don't worry if it takes you a few minutes to get through a single sentence. Once you have proven that you know and can recall the Ritual from memory the presentation will take care of itself with rehearsals.

You may find there are many parts that you can't recall and need attention. Don't be disheartened. It's better reveal them now (months in advance), rather than in the days leading up to the actual ceremony. Make sure you note them down so you know to pay extra attention to them in the future.

The benefit of working through a structured system like this ensures that you spot any areas of weakness immediately. If, as some sources recommend, you focus on the big parts you can easily let the smaller bits fall through the gaps.

Don't feel like you have to be completely word perfect by the end of this session, and don't feel like you need to say it perfectly. It's likely there will be parts you can quickly cover quickly, and other parts that need additional time and focus to get through.

The human brain is a funny object, and if you have time to go through this start of the First Degree ceremony again you'll find you'll get yourself stuck on parts you went through with ease 10 minutes before.

Today's Notes: ....

....

....

....

....

....

....

....

....

....

Day 38: First Degree Obligation Revision

After opening and getting up the First Degree Obligation yesterday, continue your revision with the First Degree Obligation (pages 81-83 in my blue book of Emulation Ritual), which was last covered on Day 33.

As with yesterday, cover the page with a piece of paper and reveal the lines after you attempt a reciting. This way you can spot any errors and correct them now – you don't want to miss a line out or get something wrong and not realise it until you are prompted in the middle of a Lodge meeting.

You may find that non-common words actually make it easier by acting as little stepping stones because they stand out. You may need to learn some pieces parrot fashion, but the uniqueness of them gives you a something to grasp.

By the end of today hopefully you can work your way through the Obligation needing only a little prompt here and there and be about 85-90% accurate.

Of the coming weeks what you have been learning will slowly fade from your short term memory; but much of it will survive in your long term memory, meaning that when it comes to preparing for an Initiation cereomy you'll be focussed on revision and rehearsal.

Today's Notes: ....

....

....

....

....

....

Day 39: Lesser Lights and Entrusting

Today you are revising what you last went over on Day 34, which combined what you first started learning on Days 24 to 27.

This covers from the end of the First Degree Obligation, up to the start of the Charge in the North East (pages 83 to 96 in my book of Emulation Ritual). Yes, it is a lot to cover! And remember, we've now moved from Learning to Revision.

This isn't rehearsal, but revision; a continuation of learning, but now you are trying to recall the text before you read it - don't feel bad about giving yourself prompts. As previously said: a piece of paper is a useful tool to cover the ritual book and slowly reveal the text once you have recited it.

If you find that you are stuck then you can easily reveal the next line to start you off. Even if you think you are correct make sure you check your accuracy regularly.

So today you are revising:

1. Post Obligation ritual
2. Lesser Lights
3. Entrusting
4. Investing with the Badge

There is a lot of work over these fourteen pages, though mercifully there is a perambulation so at least you get a short break whilst the Junior Deacon takes the Candidate to each of the Wardens, before wrapping up today's work with the presentation of the Badge.

If you have sticking points spend a little extra time on them, and if needs be revisit them again at the end of the session.

Today's Notes: ....

....

....

Day 40: Charge in the North East

I hope you have recovered from yesterday's session, today we are just looking at the Charge in the North East Part of the Lodge (pages 97-100 in my book of Emulation Ritual).

We first covered this on Day 28 and Day 29, and then had another learning session on it on Day 35 where both halves were combined.

Once you have gone through a passage check that you are correct, and if not, spend a couple of minutes working of the part you got wrong. The Charge in the North East contains a few passages where it's easy to get confused and lose your rhythm.

Remember the first half (Day 28) was broken down into six sections, and the following half (Day 29) broke down into three, and combined to:

1. Explanation of the cornerstone, and that the candidate represents it,
2. That they now stand upright (just the single sentence),
3. You'll be testing principles,
4. Explanation of charity,
5. All walks of life in Freemasonry,
6. Test principles by asking for a donation,
7. Congratulate the candidate,
8. The first and second reasons for the test,
9. The third reason.

The Charge in the North East is a very important piece of Ritual but often overlooked by new Masters who focus their efforts on learning Obligation, and leave learning this Charge until the last minute.

Today's Notes: ....

....

....

Day 41: First Degree Charter and Closing

Following the Charge in the North East we are assuming that the Working Tools will be performed by another member of the Lodge - if this isn't the case in your Lodge please allow extra time for this.

Therefore today you'll finish the First Degree ceremony and Close the Lodge. You first went through this on Day 30, and then again on Day 36.

The explanation of the Charter of the Lodge also includes giving the Candidate the Book of Constitutions and By-Laws of the Lodge; as well as letting the Candidate leave the Lodge and return (in my book of Emulation Ritual this is on pages 101-103).

You'll explain to the Candidate he needs to pay initiation fees, but before so we explain under what authority the Lodge acts. This leads to introducing the Charter of the Lodge. Remember we broke this large paragraph down into smaller chunks to aid learning.

The final paragraph is quite short and written in quite a more modern style so shouldn't be much trouble to learn, though the last couple of lines may need a couple of additional read-throughs to make it flow naturally.

Because the Charge After Initiation is usually given by a Past Master we are going straight to Closing the Lodge (pages 60-65). Like the Working Tools, if you are expected to perform this Charge allocate additional time.

This concludes your learning and revision of the First Degree Ceremony as part of this one-hundred day study plan. You've been through the ceremony twice for learning, and another as a revision. The aim of this plan isn't to get you word perfect in the First (or other) Degree, but to give you a solid foundation that means that when you do have a First Degree coming up you can spend the weeks leading up to it revising and rehearsing your delivery, not trying to learn it from scratch.

Today's Notes: ....

....

Day 42: Installation Ceremony Revision

Yesterday concluded your learning of the First Degree Ceremony, but before going onto the Second Degree Ceremony have another look at the Installation ceremony.

It was Day 31 when we last went through the Installation Ceremony, and the time before that was Day 17, so that just once in over three weeks.

After this period of time you'll want to have your book to hand. In my book Investing the Officers starts on page 214 with the IPM, then picks up with the Senior Warden on page 223, through the Offices to page 235, then Resuming is on page 68 and Closing the Lodge is pages 62-65.

As it has been over a week I would recommend that you initially skim through the Ritual first as a brief refresher. Then try and only use the book for the occasional prompt and correction, and to monitor your progress to ensure you haven't missed anything or made any errors.

You are still in the revision stage where you are building on the learning, and it's moving the Ritual from your short-term memory to your more robust longer-term memory. This doesn't mean the learning is over, but should mean that your learning is focused on areas that you have identified weakness.

There's still 59 day until your Installation, that's the best part of two months, so you have plenty of time to get the Installation Ritual perfect, and plenty of time to learn and revise the Second and Third degrees too.

Today's Notes: ....

....

....

....

Day 43: Installation Ceremony Revision – Again!

Yesterday you had your first revision of the Installation Ceremony for almost two weeks. No doubt you were a little rusty after the absence; therefore have another run through of it again today.

In my book Investing the Officers starts on page 214 with the IPM, then picks up with the Senior Warden on page 223, through the Offices to page 235, then Resuming is on page 68 and Closing the Lodge is pages 62-65.

The initial learning was putting this Ritual into your short-term memory, and when you went over it day after day it started to stick; but yesterday no doubt illustrated that with just two weeks away from it how much had slipped.

But then you probably found that after a quick review much of it came back to you, it just needed a kick start.

Even today you'll likely still needed to glance for the odd prompt and correction. You're not at the stage where you can rehearse it without the book and say it all steadily and smoothly, but don't worry, that day will come!

So to re-cap, you have learnt and revised the Installation Ceremony, plus learnt and revised the First Degree Initiation Ceremony.

Over the next fifty-seven days you'll be learning the Second and Third Degree Ceremonies, as well as spending more time revising and rehearsing for your Installation.

Today's Notes: ....

....

....

....

Day 44: Second Degree Questions

Today you will start to learn The Second Degree ceremony, but before you jump into that you will go right back to the beginning.

Start with Opening the Lodge in the First Degree (pages 42-46 in my book of Emulation Ritual), which of course you covered when learning the First Degree.

Don't skip this, it'll only take a few minutes to run through quickly; and considering every ceremony opens with this it's worth knowing you can run through the Opening without having to worry about it.

Once the Lodge is opened you would usually take items on the agenda such as the minutes of the last meeting, as well as giving salutations to visiting Provincial or Grand Officers. Let's assume this is done and turn to page 112 where the Candidate is brought up. However, the book misses out a critical line where any Entered Apprentices (apart from the Candidate) are required to leave. I suggest either:

"I must now ask any Entered Apprentices, with the exception of the Candidate, to retire from the Lodge for a short while."

Or:

"I must ask any Brother under the rank of Fellowcraft, with the exception of Brother Candidate, to retire from the Lodge for a short while."

Check with your Director of Ceremonies or Secretary to find out if there is a preference or variation in your Lodge, and if there is then make a note of it and ensure you include it in your learning.

It's better to cover minor details like this now than to try to remember such items on the evening.

The next part is the Questions to the Candidate. You should already be familiar with these from when you learnt the answers to these questions when you were the Candidate yourself, and again when you were a Deacon so you could prompt the candidate if required.

Of course, then you learnt the answers to the questions, but by learning the answers you would have familiarity with the questions; though now as Master you are taking the lead, and not responding as when you were the candidate.

It seems to be quite common for Masters to struggle with the last two questions (how do they know themselves to be a Mason, and how they demonstrate it). I believe this is because the questions are actually quite short and simple so your brain can easily switch off and forget them.

Hopefully today has been an easy session, the first half quickly running through what you already know, and the second half covering Ritual you are already familiar with.

Sometimes the trickiest part of these questions is just remembering what order they go it, so make a note of anything that will help you recall this.

Today's Notes: ....

....

....

....

....

....

....

....

Day 45: Entrusting with the Pass Grip & Word

Now the Candidate has answered the questions, today you have two pledges to ask the Candidate and Entrust them with the pass grip and pass word (pages 115-116 in my book of Emulation Ritual).

Unlike the First Degree which has three Declarations, there are two *pledges* (so no need to remember what is a promise, and what is a pledge) in the Second Degree. These are also a little shorter, and seem to flow better too; making them easier to learn.

The Entrusting of the pass grip and password is also quite short so shouldn't be too much hassle today to learn. Again, you will likely be familiar with much of this from your days as a Deacon, and also a Warden when testing the candidate.

Once Entrusted the Candidate now leaves the Lodge in order to prepare, and it makes sense to finish here for today.

Today's Notes: ....

....

....

....

....

....

....

Day 46: Second Degree Perambulations

Yesterday you Entrusted the Candidate with the pass grip and pass word before he left the Lodge room. Before he re-enters for the Passing you must Open the Lodge in the Second Degree (pages 47-50 in my book of Emulation Ritual), before commencing with the ceremony, where the candidate is re-admitted, perambulates around the Lodge and prepares for the Obligation (pages 117-128).

This is looks like quite a lot of work at first glance, but when you read through it you'll see there shouldn't be anything too strenuous – this is our first run through of this Degree so your aim is to build familiarity with the Ritual.

Let's break all of these thirteen or so pages down:

1. Opening in the Second Degree (pages 47-50) – It follows a similar format to opening in the First, but with less questions, and if you've gone through the Warden's Chairs you'll already be familiar with it.
2. Candidate enters through to Prayer (pages 117-120) – About five lines; though three of these are very short, and the other two are similar to admitting the Candidate in the First Degree.
3. First Perambulation (pages 121-123) – All done by the Senior Deacon and Wardens.
4. Second Perambulation (pages 123-126) – Only one line from the Master, and similar again to the First Degree.
5. Advancing to the East (pages 126-127) – One line from the Master, the rest is the Senior Warden and Deacon's work.
6. Pre-Obligation Preparation (pages 128) – The two biggest chunks of Ritual in today's session. The first part explains that another Obligation is required, the second gives instructions to the Candidate. This is very similar to the First Degree's preparation but the rights and lefts are switched; and the left arm is support by a Square, as opposed to being used to support Compasses.

This does look quite a bit of work, but once you cross-reference it with your own Ritual book you'll see none of this is too taxing for the Master.

You will notice that much of this requires an odd line said by the Master. I recommend reading through this pages with a high-lighter pen so you ensure you don't miss them in the future.

Sometimes the hardest part is remembering the format of the ceremony, not actually words. (This even more so in the Third Degree where you must keep track of which perambulation the Senior Deacon is on so you don't lose your place.)

Try to visualise the Lodge room and "see" what the Deacons and Wardens are doing, and don't just focus on the Master's work in isolation.

When preparing the candidate for the Obligation allow pauses for them to follow your instructions.

As ever ensure you note any areas of difficultly, or handy tips or ways to jog your memory. These notes will be invaluable in the weeks leading up to a real Passing Ceremony.

Today's Notes: ....

....

....

....

....

....

....

....

Day 47: Second Degree Obligation

Yesterday you (with the assistance of many of the other Officers in the Lodge) covered a lot of ground, from Opening the Second Degree, the perambulations, moving the Candidate to the East and preparing them for The Second Degree Obligation (pages 129-130 in my book of Emulation Ritual).

You'll be pleased to know this is the shortest of the Obligations in Craft Masonry. Because of this we won't spread it over two days as we did for the First Degree Obligation. We will of course cover it again so don't worry about learning it in just today's session.

The Obligations all have a similar format, especially the start and end of each. These similarities can actually make it harder to learn differences between them, it can be easy to drift between Degree Obligations.

You may find it useful to cross-reference between the two Obligations. Work out which parts are similar and use those as stepping-stones as you navigate through the rest of it.

1. Introduce the Lodge and VSL,
2. What they are promising to do,
3. Who/where they can communicate,
4. Pledge their responsibilities as a Craftsman,
5. Finish

It's likely that a significant proportion will be spent getting the words "regularly held, assembled and properly dedicated" in the right order.

Make notes of any ways you remember this, or any other parts of the Obligation, and how you differentiate them from the other Obligations.

Today's Notes: ....

....

....

Day 48: Second Degree Entrusting

Don't worry that you aren't word perfect with the Second Degree Obligation, I'd be very surprised if you did manage to learn it completely in just one day. You will be coming back to it for more learning and revision.

Continue you way through the Passing Ceremony today with the Second Degree Entrusting. This is quite a lot of work, and starts at the end of the Second Degree Obligation, goes through Second Degree Entrusting and concludes with the explanation of the Word (pages 130-134 in my book of Emulation Ritual).

Although it is a lot to cover, bear in mind this is your first read through of it so focus on familiarity and not beat yourself up of getting every word spot on.

Break it down into three distinct parts:

1. Post Obligation (Sealing the Obligation and position of the Square and Compasses),
2. Second Degree Entrusting (the biggest part of today's work),
3. Explanation of the Word.

Although there is a lot to cover, you'll once again see that much of today's Ritual you will recognise from when you were going through the offices. You would have already learnt most of the Entrusting and explanation of the Word as Senior Deacon.

It may be a few years since you held the Senior Deacon's office, but you'll be surprised how much of it you will be able to whizz through after just a single read through. Be careful though, there are differences.

If you didn't hold the position of Senior Deacon or you are having issues with today's work then you will need to put in a little extra work, but by the end of the session you should at least know the running order of the Entrusting.

Today's Notes: ....

....

Day 49: Charge in the South East

Yesterday covered a lot of Ritual involved in the Second Degree ceremony, going from the end of the Obligation, Entrusting with the grip and token of the Degree, and explaining the meaning of the word. This concludes with passing the Candidate (no pun intended!) over to the Senior Deacon to perambulate the Candidate again around the Lodge.

Pick things up today following the Perambulation when the Senior Warden presents the Candidate for investing with the Fellowcraft's Badge, and then giving the Charge in the South East (pages 141-143 in my book of Emulation Ritual).

The Investing with the Badge starts with a short sentence to delegate the investing to the Senior Warden, which very similar to that of the First Degree.

Once the Senior Warden has put on the apron the Master explains the future studies to the Candidate, and their duties.

The Senior Deacon then moves the Candidate in preparation for the Charge in the South East. Although this straddles two pages, it is actually about three-quarters of a page; whereas the Charge in the North East (from the First Degree) is just over one and half pages, so this one is about half the length.

In Emulation Ritual the Charge in the South East is just two sentences long. However, these sentences, especially the second one, are quite long. As with other long sentences you have encountered I recommend adding your own punctuation in order to break them down in smaller, more manageable pieces of text.

As it is common practise in the majority of Lodges for the Working Tools to be performed by a Past Master or Master Mason this course will skip it. If it is usual for the Master to do the Working Tools in your Lodge then allow extra time.

Today's Notes: ....

....

Day 50: Second Degree Closing

Today marks the midway point in your preparation as Master Elect to prepare for your year in the Chair. You have so far learnt your words and revised for the Installation and First Degree Ceremony, and today you conclude your initial familiarisation of the Second Degree Ceremony.

I know I keep saying this, but the point of these one-hundred days is to be proficient at the Ceremony you are required for your Installation, as well as get a good grounding in the three Degree ceremonies so that when your Secretary says, "next month we'll be doing a…" you have three or four weeks to brush up and rehearse, not learn!

So today you will wrap up the Ceremony of Passing with the Second Degree Closing, picking up from the end of the Working Tools.

Start with telling the Candidate they can now leave the Lodge, through to the Candidate returning and preparing for the Explanation of the Second Degree Tracing Board (pages 144-146 in my book of Emulation Ritual). There isn't much new Ritual to learn here, and what there is of it is similar to the First Degree at this stage.

Like the Working Tools, the Tracing Board is usually outsourced to a Past Master (or two, as it is a large piece) so we will skip this.

That concludes the Second Degree Ceremony itself. Now Close the Lodge, first in the Second Degree (pages 59-61) and then completely (pages 62-65).

Of course you have already covered the First Degree closing at the end of both the Installation and First Degree so concentrate your efforts on the Second Degree Closing. It is similar to the First, but there are a few questions to be addressed to the Wardens.

Today's Notes: ....

....

....

Day 51: First Half of Second Degree Ceremony

Yesterday you concluded your first run through of the Second Degree Ceremony. Now you'll go through it again, remembering that at the moment you are still in the Learning stage. You don't need to be worried about getting it word perfect or not needing any prompts. The goal is to "force" it into your short term memory with concentrated repetition, and with future revision it will then cross into your long term memory where it can be finessed at a later date.

So, today it's back to the beginning but with an increase in the pace of learning.

Before commencing the Second Degree Ceremony you need to Open the Lodge in the First, then work through the Second Degree Ceremony up to the Obligation. This is made up of the followings sessions:

1. Opening in the First Degree and Questions to Candidate (Day 44)
2. Open in Second, Pledges and Entrusting with the pass grip and word (Day 45)
3. Candidate re-enters, perambulates and goes to pedestal in preparation for the Obligation (Day 46)

In my edition of Emulation Ritual this is split between pages 42-49 for the Openings, and pages 112-128 for the first part of the Passing ceremony.

Because you are starting with Opening in the First Degree the chances are you won't need the book for this. The next part is the Questions to the Candidate. As we discussed on Day 44 you already learnt half of this when you were the Candidate yourself, then again when you were Senior Deacon so you could prompt the Candidate.

If you get some momentum going try going through it in your mind first and using the book to prompt and check your accuracy, you may be surprised.

In the process of learning there will be some pieces you are more confident with, and other areas that need more work. Make a note of them, then you can allocate additional time for these parts, forcing in the words in if need by repetition.

Slowly you'll work it into your short term memory, and then into your longer term memory with future revision.

It is very easy (and common) to focus on the parts you are confident with. This way you will feel more positive about how your learning is progressing, but this does come at a cost of neglecting the Ritual that does need work. Don't fall into this trap like so many have.

This has been quite a long session, especially if you have been having problems with it or didn't learn the answers when you were a Deacon.

Today's Notes: ....

....

....

....

....

....

....

....

....

....

....

Day 52: Second Degree Obligation

Continuing your second phase of learning the Passing Ceremony, you'll spend today looking solely at the Second Degree Obligation you first read on Day 47 (pages 129-130 in my edition of Emulation Ritual).

Look back at your notes to see if spotted any memory hooks or mnemonics to assist you. Perhaps you noted some parts that it had in common with the First Degree Obligation; or parts that are different and how you can remember those differences.

Don't feel as so you need to be word perfect straight away, but you can test yourself if you are confident. The Second Degree Obligation is quite a bit shorter that the First Degree Obligation, and borrows the same format and indeed many of the words, but with subtle differences so you may progress quicker with it that you expect.

It may pay to have a quick skim through the Obligation as a refresher before you start, then see what you can recite without the book. It is likely there are some elements (around the middle section) that will required additional attention as they are unique to this Degree.

Don't worry too much if you are getting your Obligations confused saying phrases from the First when you are doing the Second. At this point in the hundred day plan you are still learning and revising all the ceremonies so they'll all be swimming around in your mind. Once you are in the Chair you'll have a month of preparing for that ceremony exclusively.

Today's Notes: ....

....

....

....

Day 53: Second Degree Entrusting

Having finished the Obligation yesterday, the next part is the Second Degree Entrusting. You first went through this on Day 48, and starts at the end of the Obligation where the Obligation is sealed, then continue with the Second Degree Entrusting with the signs, tokens and word (pages 130-134 in my book of Emulation Ritual).

It's quite a lot of work to cover in one day's worth of learning, and we broke it into stages:

1. Post Obligation (Sealing the Obligation and position of the Square and Compasses),
2. Second Degree Entrusting (the biggest chunk of today's work),
3. Explanation of the Word.

You will recall the reason this is combined into just one session is because when you were going through the offices you will have already learnt most of the Entrusting and explanations as Senior Deacon, and also touched on it for the Wardens work too.

Talking of the Senior Deacon, once the Candidate has been Entrusted the next six or seven pages are in his hands. Remember only a few years ago these pages were an insurmountable task to learn, and now they are barely a drop in the ocean of Ritual you are learning as Master Elect!

You are still in the Learning stage so take your time working through and repeating Ritual (out loud if possible), make a conscious effort to burn the words into your mind.

Try to spend 20 minutes or so having a couple of run-throughs and focus on areas that require additional work. Do not to panic if you encounter problems along the way – time is on your side.

Today's Notes: ....

....

Day 54: Charge in the South East & Closing

You are coming to the end of your second run through of learning the Second Degree as part of this one-hundred day study guide for Master Elects. Yesterday you went from the end of the Obligation, Entrusting with the grip and token of the Degree, and explaining the meaning of the word.

This finished with the Senior Deacon taking the Candidate for a perambulation around the Lodge to meet each of the Wardens. Once the Wardens are happy the Senior Warden then presents the Candidate to the Master.

Start with Investing with the Fellowcraft's Badge, giving the Charge in the South East and finishing the Ceremony (pages 141-146 in my book of Emulation Ritual), then Close the Lodge in both Degrees (pages 59 to 65).

Remember to have a look at the notes you made on days 49 and 50 as you are now combining both those days into one session.

The Investing with the Badge starts with a short sentence to delegate the investing to the Senior Warden which essential the same to that of the First Degree, just stating the difference of Degree. Once the Senior Warden has done that you continue to explain the future study to the Candidate.

Because it is short it can be easily forgotten about. You then instruct the Senior Deacon to place the candidate in the South East part of the Lodge.

The Charge in the South East is less than a page (though it straddles two so at first looks longer than it is), and is a lot shorter than the Charge in North East you learnt for the First Degree. Even though it's shorter, it is still quite a long piece and seems devoid of punctuation so add a few commas and full stops to break it up.

Skip over the Working Tools and Tracing Board (unless you know you will have to perform them in your Lodge), then tell the Candidate they can leave to restore themselves, they re-enter, then Close the Lodge in both Degrees.

Today's Notes: ....
....

Day 55: Second Degree Ceremony Revision

Over the last eleven days you have read through Second Degree Ceremony twice. This has been what we call the "Learning" phase, where you read through the text to get familiarity and start learning it, often by repetition and spotting little acronyms to assist recall later.

The learning stage is the longest, and it is followed with revision (where you are testing yourself, but not worried about presentation; and prompts from the book are fine) and finally the rehearsal.

Today you are essentially repeating Day 51, which when you first went through the Secondary Degree Ceremony was spread over three days of learning:

1. Opening in the First Degree and Questions to Candidate (Day 44)
2. Open in Second, Pledges and Entrusting with the pass grip and word (Day 45)
3. Candidate re-enters, perambulates and goes to pedestal (Day 46)

In my edition of Emulation Ritual this is split between pages 42-49 for the Openings, and pages 112-128 for the first part of the Passing ceremony.

The Revision stage is now led by you. The way to do this is to cover what you are revising in the book, and reveal the words after you have said them – immediately checking what you have said corresponds with the actual text. This way you can correct any errors straight away and re-learn where necessary.

If you get stuck just take a breath and relax, you may surprise yourself. If you are still stuck try and take a guess; or at least remember what that part of the Ritual was about; or any key words or phrases contained in it. Should you need a prompt slide the bit of paper down a little to reveal a few words and see if this kicks things off.

Today's Notes: ....

....

....

Day 56: Second Degree Obligation Revision

Yesterday you started revising the Opening the Lodge through to preparing the Candidate for the Second Degree Obligation, which you'll spend today's whole session revising.

You first started learning the Second Degree Obligation on Day 47, and covered it again on Day 52 (pages 129-130 in my edition of Emulation Ritual).

As this Obligation is the shortest of the Three Degrees you may be tempted to focus on other areas too, but the Obligations are an important focal point of every ceremony so don't skimp on spending revision time on it.

Just like yesterday, have the book open to the page but cover the ritual. Attempt at working your way through then after a couple of lines reveal the words and check your accuracy. If you get stuck take a moment to clear your head and see if the words pop in. Should it not, or your revision isn't correct then spend a couple of minutes to focus your attention on those problem areas.

If you aren't confident doing this straight away then have a quick read through of the Obligation first, bringing it to the forefront of your mind.

You aren't rehearsing the presentation at the moment, just focus on checking your recall and working on areas that are below average standard.

Remember, you are laying the foundation for future building on, so make sure it's solid!

Today's Notes: ....

....

....

....

Day 57: Second Degree Entrusting

Having completed the Obligation yesterday there is still quite a bit of work to do in the Passing Ceremony.

Start today's session with explaining the position of the Square and Compasses, move onto the Second Degree Entrusting, finishing today with the explanation of the signs, token and word.

You first went through on Day 48 and again on Day 53. It starts at the end of the Obligation, then the Second Degree Entrusting with the signs, tokens and word (pages 130-134 in my book of Emulation Ritual).

It is quite a lot to learn and revise in one day, but remember you will have learnt quite a lot of the Entrusting and explanation of the signs and word when you were Senior Deacon and having to dictate the answers to the Candidate. You would also have covered it again when you were Senior Warden; although then you would have been asking the questions, but you would have still been revising it as part of the ritual.

This should mean that you be able to lead the way with revising, using the book for the odd prompt and correction. You'll be surprised at how much you can get through without assistance.

If you find yourself needing regular prompts feel free to skim read through the text first to bring it to the forefront of your mind to aid recall.

Today's Notes: ....

....

....

....

....

Day 58: Charge in the South East & Closing

You are coming to the end of revising the Second Degree. Yesterday you went from the end of the Obligation, Entrusting with the grip and token of the Degree, and explaining the meaning of the signs, token and word.

The Senior Deacon takes the Candidate for a perambulation around the Lodge to meet each of the Wardens. Once the Wardens are satisfied the Senior Warden then presents the Candidate to the Master.

Start today with Investing with the Fellowcraft's Badge, giving the Charge in the South East and finishing the Ceremony (pages 141-146 in my book of Emulation Ritual), finally Close the Lodge in both Degrees (pages 59 to 65).

This workbook doesn't cover the Working Tools or the Explanation of the Second Degree Tracing Board, if you are expected to perform these yourself when in the Chair ensure you allocate extra time to work on these.

This session brings to an end your third run-through of the Passing Ceremony.

Make notes of any problem areas, or solutions you found to assist you. Crucially make sure you remember to come back to these notes when you are revising and rehearsing for a Passing Ceremony when you are in the Chair.

Today's Notes: ....

....

....

....

....

Day 59: Installation Ceremony Learning

It has been over two weeks since you last revised the Installation Ceremony (Day 43) as you've been working your way through the Passing Ceremony.

It is now six weeks until your Installation. It may seem like a long time now, but I assure you it will fly by. Therefore, before cracking on with the Third Degree go back to the familiar ground of the Installation Ceremony.

You may notice from the above title that I have said "learning", not "revising" the Installation Ceremony. The reason is because of the gap you probably aren't going to be as quick and fluent as you were getting back on Day 43. No doubt you could force you way through it with several prompts and errors, but relax and use today to reacquaint yourself with it.

In my book Investing the Officers starts on page 214 with the IPM, then picks up with the Senior Warden on page 223, through the Offices to page 235, then Resuming is on page 68 and Closing the Lodge is pages 62-65.

As mentioned, today you'll use more of a refresher. Normally when learning you read the book and repeat the words yourself (i.e., the book leads), then revision you say the words before looking back in the book (i.e., you lead).

Today you will do a mixture of the two, effectively skimming over the whole ceremony. The parts that you know you can run through as quick as you like but keep an eye on the page to ensure accuracy.

On the parts where you slow down or get stuck on simply read through, and repeat a couple of times. You'll likely find this is enough to bring it back to life in your short-term memory.

Today's Notes: ....

....

....

Day 60: Installation Ceremony Revision

After yesterday's (re)Learning it should be no surprise we have another day focusing on the Installation Ceremony, only this time it is back to Revision.

Investing the Officers starts on page 214 (of my edition of Emulation Ritual) with Installing the the IPM, then picks up with the Senior Warden on page 223, through the Offices to page 235, then Resuming is on page 68 and Closing the Lodge is pages 62-65.

So now you are back in "Revision" mode. What that means is you have the book open but you lead. After yesterday's read through it should have brought this toward the front of your mind again.

You may want to cover the Ritual up with a piece of paper and check every couple of lines. It is very easy at this stage to incorporate errors or miss parts and not be aware of your error – thus ingraining them into your memory.

Try and get through as much as you can without prompting, even if it means stopping whilst you have a few deep breaths, go back a few lines and try again. If that doesn't help take a guess before going for a prompt. Check your accuracy. Would your guess have been good enough to bluff your way through?

You aren't on the Rehearsal stage yet. If you are getting word perfect then great, if you aren't then don't worry as you've still got 40 days to go.

Today's Notes: ....

....

....

....

....

Day 61: Installation Ceremony Revision

You have now spent the last two days looking at all the Ritual you need to learn ahead of your Installation Ceremony. Day 59 was more of a refresher read-though of the text, and yesterday some more focused Revision.

Before starting the Third Degree Raising Ceremony have another session today working your way through the Installation Ceremony again.

It may feel like overkill, especially if you are already confident with the Ritual and able to work your way through with only a few prompts. However, over-confidence can lead to a downfall.

When I was Installed into the Master's Chair my mind was still reeling from the Inner Workings, so when it came to Installing my Officers for the year it was good to be able to recite the Ritual on "auto-pilot" – even so I still need three prompts for the opening line for investing the Immediate Past Master!

Putting in this work ahead of time ensures your subconscious can focus on presenting the Ritual, without you getting distracted or stressed on the day.

As ever, In my book of Emulation Ritual Investing the Officers starts on page 214 with the IPM, then picks up with the Senior Warden on page 223, through the Offices to page 235, then Resuming is on page 68 and Closing the Lodge is pages 62-65.

If you are getting sick of the sight of the Installation Ritual then it shows that you are familiar with it. That's a good sign!

Hopefully you are gaining confidence with it and starting to get the stage where you are ready to start working on the Rehearsal to perfect the delivery of the Ritual.

Today's Notes: ....

....

....

Day 62: Third Degree Questions

Today you start on the final Ceremony you will learn ahead of your year in the Chair, the Third Degree Raising Ceremony.

Start today's session by opening in both the First and then Second Degree (pages 42-49 in my book of Emulation ritual), before asking the Candidate the Questions (pages 156-158).

Although you have already covered both of these Openings it's worth going through them today, even if quickly, so you can familiarise yourself with the transitions. For example, you probably sing the Opening Ode, and after the Opening in the First there may be other items your Lodge has on the Agenda before progressing to Opening in the Second.

Once the Lodge is opened in the Second Degree the Candidate is summoned. The sentences each side of the actual questions are structured similarly to the Second Degree questions.

The questions themselves you should be familiar with as you have already learnt the answers; not only when from you were the Candidate, but also from when you were the Senior Deacon so you could prompt the Candidate if required

By learning the answers you in turn had to learn the questions, at least to enough of a standard to know what each question was.

Having learnt the Second Degree you will be familiar too with the answers as many of them are taken from Entrusting the candidate in their Passing ceremony. Of course, as Master you are leading by asking the Questions.

Make a note of any issues you have, or prompts you can use to aid remembering the questions and the order they are given in.

Today's Notes: ....

....

....

Day 63: Third Degree Pledges & Entrusting

Yesterday you started on the Third Degree Raising Ceremony where you opened in the first two Degrees, and asked the Candidate the questions.

Once the Questions have been answered the Candidate affirms two pledges, and is then entrusted with the pass-grip and password leading from the Second to the Third Degree (pages 158-159 in my book of Emulation ritual).

Both of these pledges (again, not 'promises') are similar to the pledges you learnt for the Second Degree ceremony (first on Day 45). The first is pretty much identical, only now going from a Craftsman to Master Mason. The second one is exactly the same (in my book of Emulation Ritual at least!)

The Entrusting with the pass-grip and pass-word is likewise the same format as that in the Second Degree, save the obvious differences of pass-grip and pass-word. The candidate is now led from the Lodge by the Senior Deacon in order to prepare himself.

Ensure you do consciously make a note of the differences. It is very easy to skip over parts of Ritual that are similar to parts already learnt. The problem arises in the Lodge meeting when you realise you haven't actually learnt what those difference are. Trust me, it happens.

Today's Notes: ....

....

....

....

....

Day 64: Opening in the Third Degree

Over the last couple of days you have Opened the Lodge up to the Second Degree, asked the Third Degree Questions, Pledges and Entrusted the candidate with the pass-grip and pass-word.

Today involves some flicking back and forwards in the book, starting with Opening in the Third Degree (pages 50-54 in my edition of Emulation Ritual), before returning the Ceremony where the Candidate returns to the Lodge and is Perambulates around (pages 161-169).

Firstly, looking at Opening in the Third you'll see that it follows the similar format as opening in the Second Degree. One thing I find confusing here is the Master asks the Junior Warden what instruments he would like to be proved by, the Junior Warden replies and the Master doesn't then ask for this proof – it seems like the proving part itself has been edited out at some stage.

The dialogue with both the Wardens is a little confusing too. Try reading it aloud, and visualise yourself in the Chair and asking each Warden in turn their question. It's *very* easy to get out of sync – this usually happens when one or two of the Wardens are Past Masters and haven't bothered to revise this themselves. Ensure you learn the answers to each of the questions (not just the order of the questions you ask) so you immediately stop and correct any errors your Wardens may make.

Whereas you see a Lodge Opening in the First Degree at every meeting, Opening in the Third Degree only happens at Raising Ceremonies or Installations, so you probably aren't as familiar with it as you may think you are.

Once Open in the Third Degree you go back to the Raising Ceremony pages in the Ritual book where the Tyler knocks to let the Inner Guard know the Candidate is ready. You are covering eight pages of this today, but much of this work is done by the Senior Deacon interacting with the Wardens as the Candidate makes two perambulations.

Do read through this as there are a few odd lines you need to learn buried in these pages which you need to be aware of:

- Responding to the Junior Warden following the Tyler's knocks,

- Checking with the Inner Guard that the Candidate is properly prepared prior to admitting him. This is almost identical to the Second Degree ritual, but the word "propriety" is the replaced by "powerful".
- The Lodge room must be prepared. As Master you aren't directly involved in doing thing, but it is your responsibility to ensure it is correct before the Candidate is re-admitted.
- Upon his entrance you must instruct the Candidate to kneel, exactly the same as the Second.

As mentioned, much of what you are reading through today is for the Senior Deacon to learn. It is important you are familiar with it as otherwise you can easily lose where you are in the ceremony, especially in the darkness of a Third Degree which can be very disorientating for everyone involved.

The first of the perambulations is the Junior Warden testing the Candidate for the First Degree, the second is the Senior Deacon testing the Candidate for the Second Degree.

Today's Notes: ....

....

....

....

....

....

....

....

Day 65: Pre Third Degree Obligation

As this is your first reading of the Third Degree you are in the Learning stage, and your objective here is read the words and repeat them a few times to get a good familiarity with them.

Pick up today after the Perambulations and go through to the point that the Candidate is ready to start the Third Degree Obligation. (This is pages 170-176 in my book of Emulation Ritual.)

This is quite a short amount of work today; but this is the calm before the storm, because the Third Degree is going to get tougher!

The first part of this session is announcing to the Brethren that the Candidate is going to show he is prepared for the ceremony. This is similar to the Second Degree, save the inclusion of being passed to a Fellowcraft, and the Candidate is now prepared to be "Raised to the Sublime Degree of a Master Mason".

This is followed by one more Perambulation, for the purpose of proving to the Senior Warden that the Candidate is in possession of the pass-grip and password. Once happy the Senior Warden presents the candidate, and you ask him to *direct* the Deacons to *instruct* the candidate to advance to the East.

Take care as this is order to the Senior Warden is very similar to that of the former degrees, though with differences. Provincial visitors will take notice of those small details as it shows you are familiar with the whole ceremony, and that you haven't just focussed on the larger pieces such as the Obligation.

Once the Candidate is in the East you will explain another Obligation is required of them. The candidate is then instructed to get into position. Whereas in the previous Degrees you had to remember your left from right, in this Degree the Candidate kneels on both knees and places both hands on the VSL.

Today's Notes: ....

....

....

Day 66: Third Degree Obligation

You finished yesterday with the Candidate prepared to repeat the Third Degree Obligation. It is the longest of the three Obligations spanning two and a half pages (pages 176-178 in my book of Emulation Ritual).

There are some similarities to the others, and also plenty of differences. Today just concentrate on the outline. There's no point spending too much time focusing on individual words if you can't remember the structure of the piece.

Break it down into sections, and then work on each section at a time.

1. Similar to the start of the other Obligations, and includes the promise that the secrets imparted will not be disclosed to anyone who isn't a Master Mason.
2. This is a further pledge to uphold the principles and obey signs and summonses.
3. Uphold the Five Points of Fellowship, though these aren't explained until the Entrusting later in the Ceremony.
4. Maintaining the principles of a Master Mason, there isn't a similar paragraph in the other Obligations.
5. The finish the Third Degree Obligation takes you back to familiar territory, though bear in mind the differences because of the Degree.

Have a couple of read-throughs and get used to the format, you may want to break each section down further; and remember you will be pausing throughout to allow the candidate to repeat it so pencil in marks where these pauses will naturally fall.

Today's Notes: ....

....

....

....

Day 67: Revising the Installation Ceremony

Today's session marks two thirds of the way through this study plan, and leaves just over a calendar month to go.

The last few days have been spent on Third Degree, and yesterday you were looking at the Third Degree Obligation. But before continuing today you will have another quick refresher of the Installation Ceremony.

It is worth having another day on this. The Raising is a big ceremony so sneak in a quick run through of the Installation to break it up.

Today's Ritual starts on page 214 with inventing the Immediate Past Master, then picks up with the Senior Warden on page 223, through the Offices to page 235, then Resuming is on page 68 and Closing the Lodge is pages 62-65.

If you haven't already check with someone in your Lodge to see if you need to learn the extended versions of any of the other Offices, such as Chaplain, Director of Ceremonies or Charity Steward.

Even if your Lodge usually does the shorter versions, there is nothing stopping you from doing the extended versions. They don't require too much additional work as they follow the same format with the explanation the Jewel, and how it relates to the responsibilities associated with that office.

Today's Notes: ....

....

....

....

....

Day 68: Third Degree Obligation

Yesterday you had a brief departure to put in a revision of the Installation Ceremony. The day before (Day 66) you went through the Third Degree Obligation, and as it is a long piece of Ritual we'll look through it again today (pages 176-178 in my book of Emulation Ritual).

There are similarities to the other Obligations as they all follow a similar format. Hopefully by having a day away from the Third Degree Obligation your subconscious will have been absorbing it, and how it breaks down into sections:

1. Similar to the start of the other Obligations, and includes the promise that the secrets imparted will not be disclosed to anyone who isn't a Master Mason.
2. This is a further pledge to uphold the principles and obey signs and summonses.
3. Uphold the Five Points of Fellowship. (*I found this a hard paragraph as it doesn't have any parts that are familiar to the other Obligations.*)
4. Maintaining the principles of a Master Mason, and again this is a paragraph that isn't similar to other Obligations.
5. Finishing the Third Degree Obligation back in familiar territory, though bear in mind the differences because of the Degree.

Spend about five minutes or so going through each section in isolation. Read each sentence a couple of times and repeat it to yourself until you get used to it. Chances are after a couple of minutes you will forget the exact wording, but you are getting the familiarity with the ritual so you can build on it in the future.

Today's Notes: ....

....

....

....

Day 69: Post Third Degree Obligation Ritual

You've now spent a second day reading through the Third Degree Obligation. By breaking it down into its separate and distinct parts you can concentrate more manageable sections.

Today is only a little Ritual that links from the Obligation to the Exhortation (pages 178 to 179 in my book of Emulation Ritual). It's very easy to skip these parts when learning and rehearse and focus all your attention on the larger parts of Ritual, but by following this workbook it ensures all the Ritual in all the Degrees gets equal attention.

It's natural to concentrate on the "pieces" of Ritual, but if you need prompts for these transitional parts it will stand out.

The first part of today's learning is the sentence that follows the other two Obligations requiring the sealing of the Obligation, with the obvious differences to the Degree.

The second part is the paragraph that describes the position of the Square and Compasses. This is a similar format to the Second Degree. It's not just the position of them that needs explaining, but also the meaning behind that position – I actually visualise using the compass to draw a circle.

The final part is to ask the Candidate to rise, which is the same in all Degrees bar the name of the Degree itself.

Today's Notes: ....

....

....

....

....

Day 70: Third Degree Exhortation

Yesterday you covered the small piece of Ritual that leads from the Third Degree Obligation to the Exhortation (pages 180-182 in my book of Emulation Ritual), which you will now cover today.

The Exhortation in the Third Degree Ceremony is sometimes outsourced to a Past Master, but it is better if it is done by the Master himself.

When it is outsourced it may be because the Master is having problems learning all the Ritual so it is agreed with the DC to share some of the workload. If this is the case this should be decided at least a month prior to the Ceremony. This way the Brother who is tasked with performing the Exhortation has plenty of time to prepare themselves; and you know you can concentrate your revision and rehearsal efforts elsewhere.

Therefore, this workbook assumes that you are doing The Exhortation and won't skip it. If you have been told that you won't need to learn it then I suggest you still take time to read through and get familiar with the piece. You may find yourself having to do it in the future.

Either way, spend some time today reading through and getting used to it. It is approximately the same length as the Obligation, though you haven't the luxury of a standard format to follow.

In Emulation Ritual the Exhortation spreads over four large paragraphs. After a few read-throughs find the natural breaks and break it down into more manageable chunks:

Paragraph 1:
1. Following the Obligation the Candidate is entitled to secrets of the Degree,
2. Call attention to previous Degrees,
3. Distinguish and appreciate their connection.

Paragraph 2:
1. Symbolism and representation of the First Degree,
2. Benefit of charity and helping others,
3. To "bend with humility" and generally be purified.

Paragraph 3:
1. The Second Degree leads to more intellectual pursuits,
2. Unveiling the principles of nature and science,
3. Leads you to contemplate you final hour of existence.

Paragraph 4:
1. The Third Degree invites you to reflect on this,
2. Why the just and virtuous man need not fear it,
3. The noble death of HA.

This is a lot to go through. Don't feel you need to learn all of this in just one session. As already stated, read it through and break it down. Get familiar with the way the piece flows.

Make sure you make note of anything that jumps out at you that you can use as a memory hook in the future.

Today's Notes: ....

....

....

....

....

....

....

....

Day 71: Third Degree Exhortation, Again

Due to the size of the Third Degree Exhortation (pages 180-182 in my book of Emulation Ritual) spend another day trying to get to grips with it.

It is very common nowadays for pieces such as the Exhortation to be performed by a Past Master; this not only relieves the pressure on the Master, but also keeps those not holding an Office involved. Should this be the case in your Lodge still spend some time reading it through, but perhaps have a look through the notes you've kept and spend a little time working on any areas of weakness.

Yesterday you finished by breaking each of the four paragraphs down into three more manageable sections to assist with your learning. Cross reference this with any notes you made.

To be fair, learning this (even after breaking it down) is going to come down to brute force and repetition, but knowing the breakdown will help you the structure your learning. In a worst case scenario you should be able to you "busk it", or at least ad-lib a few words with confidence on the night.

Today's Notes: ....

....

....

....

....

....

Day 72: The Fifteen Fellowcrafts

Another large chunk of Ritual today: it is the part known as The Fifteen Fellowcrafts in the Third Degree Ceremony (on pages 183-188 in my book of Emulation Ritual) which follows on from the Exhortation.

Like the Exhortation it is possible that you will not have to perform this, especially if this is your first time in the Chair. However, it is technically the Master's work so do check that you are expected to do it.

It is also possible that you will perform two Raising Ceremonies during your time as Worshipful Master, and if that is the case it is likely you will be called upon to perform the whole ceremony the second time around.

Even if you aren't expected to learn it for your time in the Chair it pays to have familiarity with the piece for the future.

Knowing how the story progresses also ensures you have the understanding of the Raising ceremony as a whole. This helps move your Ritual from merely repeating the words to creating a connection with the Candidate which they will remember.

Today's Notes: ....

....

....

....

....

....

Day 73: The Fifteen Fellowcrafts, Again

Although yesterday I said it is unlikely you will be performing the Fifteen Fellowcrafts if it is your first time going through the Chair of your Lodge, it is still possible.

It would therefore be unfair to skip over such a large piece in this workbook for those that will be having to learn it for their Lodge.

Go through the piece to find your memory hooks and to break it down into easier chunks for learning. Over the last few months you have been exercising your mental muscles and should be able to apply the techniques more readily now.

If you are sure The Fifteen Fellowcrafts will be performed by a Past Master Lodge then flick through the preceding seventy-two days and skim through your notes. If there is part of Ritual you were struggling with spend another 5 minutes on it today and see how you get on.

How about picking a day or two at random and giving yourself a quick test?

Today's Notes: ....

....

....

....

....

....

Day 74: Installation Ceremony Revision

It's been a very heavy week of the Third Degree Ceremony; covering the Obligation, Exhortation and Fifteen Fellowcrafts. That is a lot of Ritual to learn, and I feel sorry for you if you are required to learn all of it.

Because of that you'll cover some familiar ground again today by looking once more at the Installation Ceremony before finishing the Third Degree off.

In my book Investing the Officers starts on page 214 with the IPM, then picks up with the Senior Warden on page 223, through the Offices to page 235, then Resuming is on page 68 and Closing the Lodge is pages 62-65.

Consider this as Revision as by now you should have learnt it, but not to perfection; the Rehearsal stage is still to come. However, if circumstances allow try and do this out loud; but not whilst driving or doing something where you can't easily refer to the book.

Keep your Ritual book close to hand for prompts and checking. It is likely that as your confidence grows you will refer to the text less and less, but this opens the door or errors to creep in.

If there are parts you confident on and consider yourself word perfect then run through those parts quickly so you can concentrate revising parts that require more attention.

Today's Notes: ....

....

....

....

....

Day 75: The Third Degree Charge

Yesterday you took a break from the Third Degree ceremony to have some revision of the Installation Ceremony, so you now continue from Day 73, which was the Fifteen Fellowcrafts.

The Charge in the Third Degree (pages 188-192 in my book of Emulation Ritual) immediately follows the Fifteen Fellowcrafts, and like that it is unlikely that you have to perform this in most Lodges, especially if this is your first time in the Chair. As ever, do check that you aren't expected to do it.

If you are going to be Master for two Raising during your year or this is your second time going through the Chair then it is more likely you'll be required to learn it. Because of that it pays to have familiarity with the piece so you aren't caught by any surprises.

Knowing how the story continues also ensures you have the understanding of the Raising ceremony as a whole, which is useful for presenting as it helps move your ritual from merely repeating the words to creating a connection with the Candidate which they will remember.

Today's Notes: ....

....

....

....

....

....

Day 76: Investing With Master Masons Badge

Continuing with the Third Degree, yesterday you read through The Charge, though this likely to be done by a Past Master (especially if this is your first time in the Chair) so you didn't spend too much time on it. Should you discover you are meant to perform these pieces yourself then make sure you allocate extra time once your Installation ceremony is out the way to work on these parts.

Start today with picking up from the end of The Charge where the candidate leaves and returns to the Lodge, and is then Invested with the Badge (pages 192-195 in my book of Emulation Ritual).

Much of this is similar to the other Degree ceremonies, and the process for the Candidate leaving and returning is the same as the other Degrees from the Master's point of view.

Similarly, when delegating the investing to the Senior Warden it is the same as the other degrees, save the description of the badge.

Once the Senior Warden has invested the Candidate with the Master Mason's Badge it again follows that the Master explains the duties of the Degree. It is a single paragraph, made up of one long sentence. Break it down a little more to assist learning it in smaller chunks.

This doesn't have much in common with the similar paragraphs in the other Degree ceremonies, so although short you may need to put a little extra work in by having a few extra repetitions of it to get familiarity with this particular piece of Ritual.

Today's Notes: ....

....

....

....

Day 77: Closing the Lodge in All Three Degrees

Today brings you to the end of your first run through of the Third Degree Raising ceremony. After today you will have covered everything you are going to need to learn ahead of your year in the Chair (barring the Inner Workings for Installing your successor).

Like in the other Degree ceremonies in this workbook you are skipping over the Working Tools in the Third Degree. In most UK Lodges these aren't usually given by the Master, but by a Master Mason getting used to doing some floor work, or a Past Master who isn't holding an office.

Of course, in the Lodge of Emulation it is done by the Master (as well as Fifteen Fellowcrafts, Traditional History and The Charge) and if you belong to a Lodge where you are expected to perform these parts then allocate extra time to learn it.

Remember, there are two objectives of this 100 Study Plan:

1. Get yourself word perfect for your Installation,
2. Get a good grip on the three Degree ceremonies.

This way when you can spend the month between each Lodge meeting revising and rehearsing for the next ceremony, not having to learn it from scratch.

Back to today, and you are going to Close the Lodge In Full through the Three Degrees (pages 54-65 in my book of Emulation Ritual).

It is very common nowadays for the Master to Resume the Lodge in the lower Degrees (particularly if it's been a long meeting) but today you will still learn the full Closing because you likely need to do it at some point during your year.

Closing in full form doesn't really take that long, so adding a minute or two onto the meeting to Close properly is probably worthwhile. Much of the work is performed by the Wardens anyway.

Today's Notes: ....

....

Day 78: The Installation Ceremony

Yesterday you completed the Third Degree by losing the Lodge through all the Degrees. That concludes your first familiarisation run through the Raising ceremony, and also means that everything you need to learn during your year in the Chair (barring the Inner Workings) you have read through at least once.

Before going through the Third Degree ceremony for a second go of learning you'll break it up by having another run through of the Installation Ceremony.

You last went through this on Day 74. In my book Investing the Officers starts on page 214 with the IPM, then picks up with the Senior Warden on page 223, through the Offices to page 235, then Resuming is on page 68 and Closing the Lodge is pages 62-65.

You are still on the Revision (not Rehearsal) stage in your preparation for the Installation Ceremony. However, try saying the Ritual out loud, as opposed to skimming through quickly in your mind or quietly under your breath.

Keep the book by you, you still have the odd bit where your mind goes blank and you need a prompt.

If possible have someone else hold the book and correct you as soon as make a mistake, and offer a prompt – but only when you request it. If that's not possible try recording yourself reciting the Ritual from memory (especially parts that you have identified as needing work) and listen back with the Ritual book in hand.

It's also worth bearing in mind anything else you need to prepare ahead of your Installation. Being a little over three weeks away you should have the received the Summons from the Lodge Secretary so make sure you have forwarded it onto your guests.

Today's Notes: ....

....

....

Day 79: The Third Degree Ceremony

Today you will start your second run through the Raising Ceremony. This is still the Learning phase so do not expect to be word perfect – especially if you are having to learn parts such as the Exhortation, Fifteen Fellowcrafts or Charge.

Bear in mind you are just getting familiarity with the Third Degree Ritual at the moment, so that when it comes to revising and rehearsing ahead of the ceremony you have a good grounding in it.

You will be covering quite a lot today, going from Opening in the First Degree, through to preparing the Candidate for the Third Degree Obligation. This covers four days from the first time through so check your notes for any tips you made.

Day 62: Opening in the First two degrees (pages 42-49) and questions to Candidate (156-158),
Day 63: Pledges and Entrusting (pages 158-159),
Day 64: Opening in Third Degree (pages 50-54) and the perambulations (pages 161-169),
Day 65: Ritual up to the Obligation (pages 170-176).

(The page numbers are based on my twelfth edition of Emulation Ritual.)

No doubt you are confident with some of these parts already, probably the first two Openings and the questions to the candidate. You will be familiar with these questions because you learnt the answers to them when you were the candidate, and probably again when you were Senior Deacon.

The rest of the Ritual leading up to the Obligation also follows the formats laid down in the previous Degree ceremonies, although there are obvious differences.

Get to grips with the structure and layout of the Ritual, and the subject of each paragraph and sentence, even if you can't remember exactly what words are used to make those sentences.

Today's Notes: ....

....

Day 80: The Third Degree Obligation

Yesterday you were learning to Open the Lodge to the Second Degree, ask the Third Degree Questions, Open in the Third and start the Raising Ceremony. This crammed four days of learning into just one session.

Today you'll focus you attention solely on the Third Degree Obligation. It spans two and a half pages (pages 176-178 in my book of Emulation Ritual). Because it is the largest of the Obligations you spent two days (Day 66 and Day 68) going over during your first run through the Raising Ceremony.

Although the format of the Third Degree Obligation follows the same standard format as the other two, you broke it down into five chunks to assist you in learning it:

1. Similar to the start of the other Obligations, and includes the *promise* that the secrets imparted will not be disclosed to anyone who isn't a Master Mason.
2. This is a *further pledge* to uphold the principles and obey signs and summonses.
3. Uphold the Five Points of Fellowship, this doesn't have any parts that are familiar to the other Obligations. It's quite long too.
4. Maintaining the principles of a Master Mason, and again this is a paragraph that isn't similar to other Obligations.
5. The finish the Third Degree Obligation is back into familiar territory, though mind the differences specific to this Degree.

Ensure you check your notes from Days 66 and 68 as you may have divided it down further or come up with acronyms to assist your recollection.

Remember you will also need to break it down even further when presenting it in Lodge so the Candidate can repeat it easily, so take this into account now.

Spend a couple of minutes on each paragraph before moving onto the next one. Then try having a run through the whole lot.

It is likely that what was almost word perfect a few minutes has now completely escaped your mind, and then when you look back at the book it seems obvious and you're kicking yourself.

It is frustrating, but it is part of the learning process.

This shows that it's still in your short-term memory, but with repetition it will slowly moving into your longer-term memory. It's not an instant process, but time spent now will pay dividends later.

Remember to note any other methods or tips you find to aid your recall. If you need a recap on these techniques have a re-read of the some of the chapters in the first section of this workbook.

Today's Notes: ....

....

....

....

....

....

....

....

....

....

Day 81: The Third Degree Exhortation

Having spent yesterday focussing just on the Third Degree Obligation you will start today with the bit of ceremony that immediately follows the Obligation that we covered on Day 69 (pages 178-179 in my book of Emulation Ritual) before going onto the Third Degree Exhortation covered on Days 70 and 71 (pages 180-182).

The Ritual that follows the Obligation is quite short and mainly focuses on sealing the Obligation and the position of the Square and Compasses. Remember that now the both points of the compasses are visible they can be used to draw a circle.

The Third Degree Exhortation doesn't follow any format from the other Degrees so it's four paragraphs must be learnt by repetition and generally forcing it in.

Not all Worshipful Master's perform the Exhortation, especially if it their first year in the Chair.

If you are not expected to learn the Exhortation look through any notes you made from the Obligation and see if there are areas that require more work to learn.

Should you be required to learn the Exhortation for your year in the Chair then look back at Day 70 where it detailed breaking the Exhortation down into more manageable chunks and discussed how the piece is structured and formatted.

Today's Notes: ....

....

....

....

....

Day 82: Master Mason Badge and Closing

Continuing with the Third Degree, yesterday you went from the end of the Obligation and through the Exhortation.

On your first run through the Raising Ceremony you covered the Fifteen Fellowcrafts and the Charge. We discussed that it is unlikely you'll be performing these if it's your first time in the Chair, or at least your first time doing this ceremony; so therefore this workbook won't cover those in much more detail.

If you are required to do either, or both, of those pieces then schedule additional time to learn, revise and rehearse them once you have finished with workbook and been Installed.

Start today's session with picking up from the end of the Charge where the candidate leaves and returns to the Lodge, is then Invested with the Badge (pages 192-195 in my book of Emulation Ritual). Following the Charge is the Working Tools, and like the Fifteen Fellowcrafts and Charge this workbook assumes this will be done by another member of your Lodge.

Once the Working Tools have been presented move to Closing the Lodge (pages 54-65), although it is possible you will Resume (page 68) in the lower degrees to save time.

As mentioned previously, much of this is similar to the other Degree ceremonies where the Candidate is told they can retire from the Lodge.

Once the Senior Warden has invested the candidate with the Badge of a Master Mason it again follows with the Worshipful Master explaining the duties of the degree. It's only a single paragraph (actually it's one long sentence), but it can be a little tricky to learn so benefits breaking it down (see Day 76 for a reminder).

It is worth ensuring you are up to speed with Closing the Third and Second Degrees in full too.

Today's Notes: ....

Day 83: Revising the Installation Ceremony

Having finished your second run through the Third Degree Raising Ceremony we will once again have a refresher of the Installation Ceremony.

In my book Investing the Officers starts on page 214 with the IPM, then picks up with the Senior Warden on page 223, through the Offices to page 235, then Resuming is on page 68 and Closing the Lodge is pages 62-65.

You are probably up to speed with the Installation ceremony but as it is now a little over two weeks away it is no-doubt coming to the forefront of your mind. Fellow Masons are likely asking if you are prepared, not to mention the pressure you are probably putting on yourself. After all, you've been a Freemason for over seven years, and those hours spent learning Ritual and attending Lodge of Instruction feels like it is all leading to the moment you will be put into the Chair of King Solomon.

If you can start your time in the Chair by Investing your officers with confidence, and run the Lodge with decorum straight away it will do wonders for your confidence over the coming year.

And that's why this workbook focuses so much on getting that first 30 minutes of the year ahead right!

As you are no doubt getting used to doing, go through the Installation Ceremony without the book to hand. When you get to a point you stall at spend a couple of seconds to remember it. If you don't need a prompt but have the feeling that a piece of Ritual doesn't feel right make a note, but continue on so you don't lose your flow.

Once you've gone through the ceremony take a look at your notes and concentrate on those parts, and see how you handle those pieces again. If you still get stuck on them, or it still doesn't feel right now cross-reference those parts with Ritual book, and ensure you focus on correcting them.

Now work your way through those areas you made a note of again. How did you get on this time? Did you go through it effortlessly after you reminded yourself or did you still get stuck or fumble over the words?

If so highlight these sticking points and make them a priority to learn. It is very easy to go through the Ritual you know and avoid the Ritual you don't.

One technique I found that worked well was to put small book-marks made from thinly torn strips of Post-It Note in my Ritual book so I could quickly turn to a part that needed a little extra work when I had a spare five minutes free through-out the day.

Once you feel confident with each area you remove the book-mark, and you'll gain confidence as you visibly see the number of book-marks reduce.

Of course this technique works well for all the Degree ceremonies too.

Today's Notes: ....

....

....

....

....

....

....

....

....

Day 84: Installation Ceremony Problem Areas

Yesterday you went through the Installation without your Ritual book to hand for prompts and noted areas that required work. You went through these areas again and highlighted those shortlisted where problems still arose.

Today, instead of going through the whole Installation ceremony just look at your notes and run those all those areas you had listed (without the Ritual book) and see how you get on.

You may have already highlighted these areas in your Ritual book with scraps of paper or Post-It Notes as book-marks.

Were any of those "blips"? It's surprising how a piece of well learnt Ritual can disappear from your mind one day and return perfectly the next. I guess this has something to do with your brain relocating it from your short- to long-term memory banks.

Do problems arise again in the parts you highlighted yesterday? If so really make these parts a priority. Even going into a ceremony knowing there are just a couple of lines you aren't sure on can really play on your mind and affect how you perform the rest of the Ritual. (Subconsciously you know you will be making errors, so you'll likely make errors in the Ritual you actually do know.)

Once the Ritual is safely in your long-term memory you can safely leave the book alone, confident that we have the correct words stored in our mind and concentrate your efforts on Rehearsing.

Note areas that you still have trouble with. Place small bookmarks in your Ritual book where these parts are and carry the book around with you. Every time you have a couple of spare minutes through-out the day grab the book, open to one of these pages and test yourself.

Today's Notes: ....

....

....

142

Day 85: Revising the Raising Ceremony

Following two read-throughs of the Raising Ceremony to get familiarity and Learn the Raising Ceremony Ritual, you will today start your third go through. Your first two run-throughs were what we classed at the Learning stage, and you are now on the Revision stage. What this means is now you are going to build on what you have already worked on learning.

Because the Third Degree is such a long ceremony we will still break it up into more manageable chunks to fit within your daily sessions. Today you will start with Opening in the First Degree, through to the Third Degree Obligation.

You last went through this on Day 79, when it was condensed down from:

Day 62: Opening in the First two degrees (pages 42-49) and questions to Candidate (156-158),
Day 63: Pledges and Entrusting (pages 158-159),
Day 64: Opening in Third Degree (pages 50-54) and the perambulations (pages 161-169),
Day 65: Ritual up to the Obligation (pages 170-176).

Go through your notes of each of these days, and Day 79 as you may have made a record of an acronym or mnemonic to assist you at any stage.

Now you are on the Revision stage you should be familiar with the order of the ceremony and Ritual you'll be saying, though not necessarily with great accuracy. Don't worry too much about being word perfect, or spending too long testing yourself.

It is important though to keep track of the perambulations. It's likely been a few years since you were Senior Deacon so still read through and absorb this.

Have your Ritual book open and on the page but keep it covered with a piece of paper, reveal it and check your progress every couple of sentences. If you are accurate, or at least close, feel free to move onto the next part. Parts that you don't know, or parts that you had issues with spend a bit more time working on it.

Should you get to a point where you are drawing a blank feel free to remove the paper and not only get a prompt, but remind yourself of a whole section. Make sure you note this down though for future revision.

After a couple of minutes you may well be word perfect, but after a while this is likely to slip. This is the process of building it in the short-term memory, and it takes time to build this in the long term-memory.

Remember that this workbook isn't designed to get you word perfect in this, or the other Degree ceremonies. It will however give you a very solid foundation so that when you are in Chair you are prepared for the coming Ceremonies so that you can Revise and Rehearse them in the weeks leading up to them.

Today's Notes: ....

....

....

....

....

....

....

....

....

Day 86: Revising the Third Degree Obligation

Yesterday you started your third run through the Raising Ceremony, and you have now moved from the Learning to Revision stage of the process.

Yesterday you Opened the Lodge to the Second Degree, asked the Third Degree questions to the candidate, Opened to the Third Degree and continued the Raising Ceremony (which mostly falls to the Senior Deacon to lead the Candidate in the perambulations) culminating in bringing the candidate to the East in preparation for the Obligation (pages 176-178 in my book of Emulation Ritual).

If you recall when you went through the Third Degree Obligation (Days 66, 68 and 80) you broke it down into sections to aid memorisation. These were:

1. Start of Obligation,
2. Pledge to uphold the principles and obey signs and summonses,
3. Five Points of Fellowship,
4. Maintaining the principles of a Master Mason,
5. Finish the Obligation.

As this is the revision stage try remembering each sentence or section first before checking it against the book. Make an effort to learn the correction by repeating it a few times before trying again.

However, if you find that hard to do straight away have a quick skim through the whole Obligation at the start of the session. Sometimes that is all that is needed, it's almost like your brain just needs to load the relevant data files in from a back-up drive (your long term memory).

I found visualising Closing in the Third Degree in full form (from when I was a Warden) helped with remembering the order of the Five Points of Fellowship.

Today's Notes: ....

....

....

Day 87: Revising the Third Degree Exhortation

Continue your Revision of the Third Degree Ceremony today with the Exhortation. It follows the Obligation that we first covered on Day 69 (pages 178-179 in my book of Emulation Ritual) before going onto the Third Degree Exhortation on Days 70 and 71 (pages 180-182).

On your second read through of the Third Degree those days were combined into Day 81.

Once the Obligation is complete the next Ritual seals the Obligation and explains the position of the Square and Compasses, you should be relatively familiar with this part as it follows a similar format as in the Second Degree.

Moving onto the Exhortation, as I've said previously the only way around this is to learn it! It doesn't follow any formats that you've encountered elsewhere. The only compensation is it more of a "story" and has a more modern feel to the text than some of the Ritual.

It has been a week since you last went through the Exhortation so if you are having problems instead of getting frustrated have a quick read through it first, then try again. I'm sure you'll be surprised how it starts coming back to you.

Don't worry on achieving accuracy. When working your way through hopefully you can give a good outline of each sentence, preferably using many of the correct words.

Any parts that you do get stuck on ensure you spend a little extra time repeating a few more time. If you can find any memory hooks or systems to aid your recall make sure you make a note of them so you don't forget them in the future.

Today's Notes: ....

....

....

Day 88: Revising The Badge and Closing

You are at the final day of your third run through (the Revision stage) of the Third Degree in this one-hundred day workbook, therefore you'll complete the Raising Ceremony by presenting the Master Mason's Badge and Closing the Lodge.

You'll start today with picking up from the end of the Charge where the candidate leaves and returns to the Lodge, then Invested with the Badge (pages 192-195 in my book of Emulation Ritual). Following the Charge is the Working Tools, and like the 15 Fellowcrafts and Charge; we are assuming this will be done by another member of your Lodge and hence has only been covered briefly in this workbook.

Once the Working Tools have been presented move on to Closing the Lodge (pages 54-65), although it is possible you will Resume (page 68) in the lower degrees to save time.

By now you should be able to run through the words (or at least have a good punt at them) before checking for accuracy with the book.

With regard to the Closing, it's worth going through the Closing in Full Form just to be sure, you don't want to get caught out; though much of the work involved in Closing in Full Form is done by the Wardens who conferred the substituted secrets to you.

Well done for making it through the Raising Ceremony. It is by far the longest of the Degrees, even after assuming that quite a bit of this will be outsourced to Past Masters or Master Masons. If you haven't already check exactly what Ritual you will be expected to perform, and adapt further revision and rehearsal of the Third Degree to suit your Lodge's interpretation of the Ritual.

Today's Notes: ....

....

....

Day 89: Revising The Installation Ceremony

Over the preceding eighty-eight days you have been through each of the three Degree ceremonies three times. The first time was at a slow methodical pace to allow you to absorb the Ritual and get familiar with it, the second time picked up the pace of Learning. The third time was Revision so you could see what framework you had learnt and focus on building the Ritual around it.

You have also gone through the Installation Ceremony many times, and as that is now the next ceremony you'll be involved in it makes sense to come back to it again today.

In my twelfth edition of Emulation Ritual Investing the Officers starts on page 214 with the IPM, then picks up with the Senior Warden on page 223, through the Offices to page 235, then Resuming is on page 68 and Closing the Lodge is pages 62-65.

You will soon be entering the Rehearsal stage, this is where it is assumed you have effectively learnt all of the Ritual required of you and can work on your performance and presentation. Before you do that you want to do some final checks to ensure you have learnt it correctly.

This time keep your Ritual book closed, but to hand in case you do need it. If possible go for a walk and see if you can recite all you need to in your mind or under your breath.

The benefit of walking (as opposed to driving) is it is easier to reference the book if required. There's also the health benefits, which no doubt you'll need from all the festive boards you'll be attending during your year!

Today's Notes: ....

....

....

....

Day 90: First Degree Revision

You will soon be focusing exclusively on Rehearsing for your Installation ceremony, but before doing that take your mind off it by seeing if you can go through a complete First Degree ceremony in your mind.

It was a long time ago, in fact the last time you Revised the First Degree ceremony as part of this course was on Days 37 to 41 – and it was spread over five days.

Before starting read through any notes you made, no doubt there will be a few things that jog your memory that you would have otherwise forgotten.

See how you get on. It is good to have a refresher once in a while.

You'll be surprised at how much you can remember, and also by how much you have forgot – but will likely remember after a prompt.

This demonstrates how following this workbook is moving the Ritual into your long-term memory. Not only will you enter your year in the Chair with a tremendous advantage, it will also be a great benefit through-out the rest of your Masonic career where you may be asked to stand-in, prompt or even teach and mentor Master Masons going through the Offices themselves.

You should also see that when you need to perform a First Degree ceremony it should only take a couple of weeks of Revision and Rehearsal to get up to speed with it – as opposed to trying to learn it from scratch.

Today's Notes: ....

....

....

....

Day 91: Revising The Installation Ceremony

Have another go at going through the whole Installation Ceremony again, just as you did on Day 89.

Again, try and do this without referencing the booking unless you really do get stuck or you are sure you have made an error.

Hopefully you will feel that you could recite the ceremony with only a few little errors here and there, and those probably wouldn't have been noticed by many but the most proficient Ritualist.

You may find there are still parts which throw up difficultly; such as when Investing the Deacons the "care and attention" sentence is different, yet similar for both the Senior and Junior Deacon.

After managing to get much of the Installation ceremony complete without referencing the Ritual Book (don't worry if you did, there's still time to polish it up) you should be feeling confident. This is important because it means you can focus your energies on presentation, not worrying about whether you are correct.

Remember to keep a note of how you got on.

Today's Notes: ....

....

....

....

....

Day 92: Second Degree Revision

Just like Day 90 when you Revised the whole of First Degree, you are going to do the same again today but for the Second Degree Passing Ceremony.

The last time you Revised this Degree was over Days 55 to 58, which spread it over four days. Similar to the other day you will go through it all in just today's sessions, and hopefully from memory.

Of course, before starting read through any notes you made on Days 55 to 58, as well as previous days when you were learning it. There may have been a good acronym you came up with to assist your recollection.

Don't feel like you need to attempt to go through it all without the book to hand like you have been doing recently with the Installation ceremony. There is a lot less required of you as the newly Installed Master in an Installation ceremony as compared to a Degree ceremony, plus this workbook has made preparation for your Installation the priority.

Again, you should see that large pieces of the Ritual that you had never looked at a couple of months ago are now embedded into your memory, and with a little more Revision and Rehearsal closer to the time will make your preparation a lot less stressful.

Because you have recently completed the Third Degree Raising Ceremony you won't be coming back to it again in this workbook as you'll now be focussing on your upcoming Installation. It is recommended though that you have regular revision session on all the Degree ceremonies through-out your year.

Today's Notes: ....

....

....

....

Day 93: IPM & Wardens Rehearsal

For quite a while now you have been revising the Installation Ceremony in one go, but today you are going back to splitting it up. This is because you are now entering the final Revision stage of learning the Masonic Ritual.

Now you are confident we have the words securely in your mind (barring the occasional lapse) you are ready to start working on the presentation aspect. You'll see that often the best Ritualists are those that don't sound like a robot reciting the Ritual word for word, but those that communicate the meaning behind the Ritual with understanding.

To achieve this you need to start saying it out loud. Don't just mumble the Ritual quietly under your breath, but properly say it; and if possible, projecting it just as you would in Lodge.

Of course, this may not be practical, so some adaption may be required.

For example, if you live in flat you don't want to be waking the neighbours if you rehearse late at night or early in the morning. However, as you no longer need the book you can rehearse whilst in the car, and with hands-free kits anyone looking at you in their rear-view mirror will just assume you are talking on the phone.

Of course, if you use public transport rehearsing on your morning commute probably isn't that suitable so look at your daily routine to find when you can accommodate 'noisy' rehearsal sessions.

If you are self-conscious then try to find a quiet spot by yourself where you can still comfortably talk at a normal level. Although you may not be projecting your voice, ensure you talk at a similar speed to as you would in Lodge.

It helps greatly to try to visualise yourself in Lodge, and visualise yourself going through the actions of Investing with the Wardens with their jewels; and pausing whilst you put the collars over their heads. You are mentally acting out the Ritual, not just reciting the words.

You'll find that going through as Rehearsal is different to Revision. Often a mistake people make is to skip the rehearsal, and rely on revision, thinking that being confident in the words is all that's needed.

Being in a full Lodge room with all the members of the Lodge, their guests, your guests and no doubt a couple of senior members of your Province looking at you really puts the pressure on.

Visualising this, your actions and hearing the sound of your own voice will go some way to preparing for this.

Today's Notes: ....

....

....

....

....

....

....

....

....

....

Day 94: Deacons and Officers Rehearsal

Yesterday you moved from Revision to Rehearsal. You just went through the Installation of the Immediate Past Master and the Senior and Junior Wardens, today we continue with Rehearsing the Installation of the Deacons and remaining Officers of your Lodge.

As with yesterday you are leaving the book aside and relying on all the Learning and Revising of the Ritual to see you through.

Continue through the rest of the ceremony and then Close the Lodge. As you have been covering Closing in full in all three Degrees as part of the Raising Degree you should be up to speed with this, hence why it is included in today's session.

As with yesterday; try and do this out loud if you can, and at the same speed you'll be talking in Lodge. Also remember to allow pauses for putting on the collars, acting out the actions if you can – especially when presenting the Tyler with his sword.

Should your Installation be tomorrow then you may not be completely prepared, but you'd be able to do what's required to get the job done. But relax, it's not tomorrow, you still have a week left.

Today's Notes: ....

....

....

....

....

Day 95: Rehearsing the Installation Ceremony

Yesterday you completed a Rehearsal of your approaching Installation Ceremony, which was spread over two sessions so you could concentrate on the presentation aspect.

Today you are going over it again, but rehearsing all of the parts you'll need to be presenting.

You may find you still need the occasional prompt, but you'll likely see that these are more random occurrences. Should you get stuck or slip up at a certain place more than once pop a bookmark in your Ritual book and over the coming days spend a few quiet minutes focussing on just those parts.

It may be that you found the Revision stage quite easy and could rapidly progress through the ceremony in your mind, but now you are Rehearsing out loud you are losing your place. This can also be down to the change of pace as you are processing the upcoming information at a different speed than you are used to.

This really illustrates the importance of Lodge of Instruction and Lodge rehearsals, and why you must Rehearse properly.

You should also have the Summons for the Installation meeting which includes the agenda. Incorporate this into your Rehearsal too. This way you know what to say when going through the Risings, collecting alms or any other Lodge business that needs to be conducted.

As well as the words themselves, get familiar with when to gavel, and waiting for the Wardens to complete their gavels before proceeding with the item.

Today's Notes: ....

....

....

Day 96: Visit an Installation & Write Ad-Libs

If possible arrange to visit an Installation ceremony today, or in the next few days. Even it is too late to book yourself in for the Festive Board you should still be able to attend the ceremony itself.

Don't just sit back and passively watch the ceremony, but try and keep track of the Ritual and quietly mouth along with the ceremony.

It is also a great opportunity to see what you have been learning over the last couple of months and watch it being performed live in front of you. Take notice of the actions, not just the words, as well as paying attention to any differences this Lodge has in comparison to your Lodge workings.

If you are unable to attend an Installation ceremony today make sure you at least have another Rehearsal, following the same format as yesterday.

It is also customary that after each Investiture the new Master says a few words to each of the Officers after the Ritual. These are usually ad-libbed and go along the lines of thanking them for taking on the role and wishing them a good year.

Although you don't need to write and learn word for word what you will say to each, I do recommend spending a moment today going through each office and working out what you will say to each person. Something unique and heartfelt will come across a lot better than repeating the message for each.

For example, if it's a Master Mason who is progressing through the ranks then praise them on their progression and wish them well in their new Office, and encourage them to work through the rest of the Offices until they are Installed into the Chair themselves.

Perhaps one of your Wardens is nervous now they see they are getting closer to the Master's Chair themselves; so acknowledge this and tell them they'll have a good year ahead, and to use the time wisely!

If it's a Past Master then thank them for stepping in and holding an office for the year.

Think of it this way; if you ever see a stand-up comedian they will often be quick witted and respond to comments and heckles quickly. These are referred to as ad-libs and are things they say off the top of their head. You'll often hear people say that a comedian is very quick witted coming up with these responses.

In reality these comments are rarely improvised on the spot, but have been prepared for when the situation arises (and what appears as a one-off event can actually happen quite regularly). It is wise you do a similar thing and at least have a brief outline for each Officer, and make them different and personal to each one being invested.

Although they are said to just the one person, they will be audible to everyone else in the Lodge room, and as you'll be leading these Officers in the coming year it pays to start off on a positive footing with each.

Today's Notes: ....

....

....

....

....

....

....

....

....

Day 97: Speak Like Churchill, or Jim Hacker?

Yesterday you rehearsed the Installation Ceremony (and maybe even attended a real one) as well as least planned what you will say to each Officer after you have invested them with their collar.

Today you'll have another full rehearsal of the Ritual you'll be saying in the Installation, but paying particular attention to how you are saying it. Pretend to speak like Winston Churchill, or at least like Jim Hacker.

Ok, what the heck do I mean there? Let me explain, especially for any non UK based Freemasons, or those who are under 40.

Basically, when you are performing ritual in Lodge then you need to "perform" it, not look like you've learnt it parrot fashion from the book. This is traditionally cited as the mark of a good Ritualist – even more than correctness. Ritual that has a sense of drama to it conveys importance and gravitas. It grabs the attention of those listening, and it draws them in.

A way to achieve this is to imitate the style of Churchill when he gives a speech. This isn't a known tip, or even one that someone has suggested to me, but a little quirk that I spotted when watching an episode *Yes, Minister* (a 1980's British sit-com set in the Houses of Parliament, with Minister Jim Hacker as the central character).

If you ever listen to any of Churchill's speeches he talks slowly and with gravitas. He pauses, adds emphasis on some words. Sentences build with intensity, then drop again. His speech is measured and controlled, with a slow tempo, yet that tempo fluctuates.

Listen to one of his famous speeches at *www.in-the-chair.co.uk/churchill*.

Coming back to *Yes, Minister;* whenever Hacker had visions of grandeur he would speak in a way that reflected his hero, Churchill.

Watch a short clip here: *www.in-the-chair.co.uk/hacker*.

Therefore, when rehearsing the ritual today, do it as so you are doing an impression of Winston Churchill. It will feel odd, but try to embrace the role and add some Churchill-isms. You may be surprised how by just imitating Churchill you (like Jim Hacker) have added depth and solemnity to the Ritual.

You may surprise yourself at just how effective this technique is, especially if you have a tendency to rush through the Ritual in Lodge. Of course you don't want to do this for the whole ceremony, but taking aspects of it in moderation will no doubt help bring additional depth to your Ritual.

Of course, it is well known that Churchill was Freemason, and it makes you wonder what being in a Lodge whilst Churchill delivered ritual would have been like.

Today's Notes: ....

....

....

....

....

....

....

....

....

....

Day 98: Write Your Speech Festive Board

It's now just a few days until you are Installed into the Chair of King Solomon, and no doubt everyone is reminding you of that fact.

Yesterday you rehearsed the Installation Ceremony again, and tried an exercise in presentation by attempting to emulate the style of Winston Churchill. Admittedly a little odd, but hopefully you found it useful.

Today run through the investiture of all your officers again (including any personal comments after each investiture), other items on the agenda and Close the Lodge. You should be in a position where you can run through this whilst driving or going about other daily tasks.

Remember the evening isn't just about the ceremony itself; there is also the Festive Board afterwards, so today you will allocate time to prepare yourself for this aspect of the evening too.

There are toasts that will be made, but these will be prompted by the Director of Ceremonies or Immediate Past Master, though if you have an opportunity to read through the toast list prior to it a little familiarity won't hurt, especially if you are reading names and titles that may an odd pronunciation.

"It usually takes me more than three weeks to prepare a good impromptu speech" – Mark Twain

Prepare the speech you will give at the Festive Board, so often this is forgotten about and the new Master jots down a few notes during the course of the meal. This usually includes a badly told joke he heard when he visited another Lodge.

Avoid going the complete other way and completely scripting it and reading it verbatim, as some also do. Make some bullet points of what you want to cover, such as people you want to thank (proposer, seconder, visitors and those that have helped you in your Masonic career) as well as mention the dates of Ladies Nights, White Tables or any other social events you have during the coming year.

And aim to keep your speech between three and five minutes long.

You'll need your own note-book for today!!!

Day 99: Start to Panic...

Only a few days to go!

Yesterday, as well as rehearsing the Installation ceremony, you also outlined your speech for the Festive Board.

Make sure you are rehearsing properly and not rushing, but try to do it at the pace you would perform on the evening; and out loud (even if not projecting as loudly as you would).

As well as the Ritual in the book remember what you want to say to each of the Officers after you have invested them with their collars, which you covered on Day 96.

Go through the full Agenda of the meeting, and ensure you rehearse such items as reports from the various Officers before the Raisings and Closing the Lodge. If there are any ballots ensure you know the procedure your Lodge follows, check with the Secretary who will be happy to go through it with you.

Finally, run through the agenda for the Festive Board, ensuring you are familiar with the toasts you will be proposing; as well as a brief run through of your speech that you will be making. Remember that it will have been a long evening so keep it short and concise, and no more than five minutes!

After all these years working through the Offices, time spent learning, revising and rehearsing, not to mention all those evenings attending Lodge of Instruction it's natural to start feeling a little anxious.

But all the hard work you've been putting in over the last ninety-nine days should mean you are as prepared as you possibly could be, and probably more so than anyone else in your Lodge will have been ahead of their year in the Chair.

Today's Notes: ....

....

Day 100: Good Luck

Day 100 out of 100, and your Installation is tomorrow.

Yesterday you pulled together all the final parts for your Installation Ceremony, including the speeches and other parts of the Festive Board.

You probably don't need telling that today you should get in the odd rehearsal or two, and to run through your duties at the Festive Board. It's also a good idea to make sure your suit is ready, your shirt ironed and shoes are polished so you aren't faffing tomorrow afternoon.

Well done for making it through the last one hundred days, it has taken real dedication to stick with this workbook; but it is inevitable that all your hard work will pay off.

Over this time you have fully prepared and rehearsed for every aspect of your Installation. As well as that you have also learnt and revised the three Degree ceremonies you'll be performing during your time in the Chair.

This course deliberately finishes the day before your Installation so that tomorrow you can get on with your day as normal and go to your Installation meeting without any last minute worries.

After tomorrow you can relax knowing you are the Worshipful Master of your Lodge, and the day after that it will be time to start revision and rehearsal ahead of your first full ceremony the following month!

Good luck once again, and enjoy it!

Please let me know how you get on, I'd love to hear how you get on. Drop me an email (*robert@in-the-chair.co.uk*) and tell me how it goes. It's been a pleasure to accompany you on your journey to the Chair, and I hope this is just the start or your journey that continues for many years to come.

The best of fraternal wishes,

Robert Bone

Useful Links

In The Chair Blog: *www.in-the-chair.co.uk*

In The Chair, The Masonic Podcast: *www.masonicpodcast.com*

Buy "Learning Masonic Ritual" by Rick Smith on Amazon:
www.in-the-chair.co.uk/learn

Rick Smith's interview on the podcast: *www.masonicpodcast.com/3*

Robert's Magician Site (entertainment for your ladies night!):
www.robertbone.co.uk

Printed in Great Britain
by Amazon